Beautiful THINKING

Wisdom, Courage and Grace

TRICIA GREENWOOD

Cover Photo: Mel Lindstrom Photography
Photo on Cover: Tricia Greenwood
Photo of Tricia on Back Cover: Mel Lindstrom
Publisher: HeartSpeak Publishing
Editor: Hamilton Wordsworth
LCCN: 20179113869
ISBN: 978-0-9978798-8-9
www.heartspeakpublishing.com
email: admin@heartspeakpublishing.com
Printed in USA

Contents

HeartSpeak

Introduction

We could all use more wisdom, knowledge and confidence in the world we live in. Those who have lived before us have written books that have much to offer on inspiration and philosophy. You will discover timely words of wisdom from some of my favorite authors that I have taken artistic license with by interweaving their written words with mine.

The Authors I chose are from books written and popular in the previous century as well as today. The names of the authors I chose to include are in the Bibliography at the end of this book.

I want to share with you these tried and true methods of doing and thinking I have studied since I was a teenager to attain peace and live a happier life. I hope your sorrows are few and you will be someone who can overcome your life's obstacles and become victorious. It has been said that there is no beautifier of complexion, or form, or behavior like the wish to spread joy. If your eye is on the eternal, your intellect will grow. Your opinions and actions will have a beauty which no conventional learning or perceived advantages can rival.

Beauty is the form under which our intellect prefers to study the world. All privilege is that of beauty, for there are many types of beauty, those of our nature, of our face and form, of manners and moral beauty. Then there is Beautiful Thinking, which is the beauty of the heart, mind and soul.

Goethe said, "Beauty is a manifestation of secret natural laws, which otherwise would have been hidden from us forever."

Until now...

It's worth mentioning that the first chapter of this book, "Inner Beauty", is also the LAST chapter of my book titled, "Frazzle to Dazzle". It could even be said that a major motivator for writing this book is much attributed to the welcomed commentary and feedback I have received from many readers of "Frazzle to Dazzle".

Beautiful Thinking would not have been complete without this chapter on "Inner Beauty" to emphasize the importance of "priorities" when it comes to presenting one's self to others.

To assume that "beauty" is something confined to the "superficial", is to miss entirely the very nature of its meaning.

It is my sincere hope that sharing my experiences, knowledge, truth, and wisdom interwoven with the words of Authors who previously left their mark on the world, will help empower you to overcome life's obstacles and achieve your goals, big or small, humble or grand, and "see" the beauty in all things.

Inner Beauty

As within...
Beauty that comes from within is the only kind that will last. So how does one have inner beauty that lasts through the years?

By having a heart that loves and understands, a heart and mind that forgives without keeping a record of wrongs.

By having faith and believing that you were born with a purpose, realizing what that purpose is and fulfills it.

When you have confidence, the kind of confidence that does not need to compare what you may or may not have, or how your body or looks compare with other people. We are all unique.

Undeniable Beauty is perceived and appreciated by all of us. It is how humans are "wired". Here are some helpful observations to share with you...

Watch out for these often overlooked "basics" that can undermine your desire to present the Inner Beauty that is YOU.

Being competitive or jealous breeds anger, shame, and guilt that can rob one of their inner beauty and peace.

The media does a great job of instilling these worthless values in the general public through advertisements, TV, and movies. If competition only existed in sports I think life would be much sweeter.

As far as music and art, I believe it's considered to be subjective.

The discoveries in science are always new and theories have to be proven to be fact. The kind of inner beauty I want to tell you about is the kind that gives you peace and does not entertain thoughts of fear and negativity.

Be mindful of what occupies your mind.

I like reading books on philosophy, psychology, and religion. I own books I can learn from and share my knowledge with others to help their understanding in human relationships.

What an opportunity to share wisdom and knowledge while I have a client sitting in my chair at the salon for an hour or two while I beautify them.

For me the most important thing in the world is Love. A child is born with innocence and learns what they live. DNA generates many factors in a personality but can be artfully molded into the beauty of patience, caring, and truth.

A loving spirit can change the temperature in a room and create waves of positive energy. I always say, "You can steal my parking place but not my joy".

So how do you overlook the negativity you might feel when confronted with the person looking you up and down in the grocery line or the relative that has a way to push your buttons and upset you, stealing your joy?

No one is perfect and there will be times when your armor is down and you get attacked or confronted without warning and react in a less than caring way. Forgive yourself and the other person and move on from it.

"The beauty of a woman must be seen from in her eyes because that is the doorway to her heart, the place where love resides."
- Audrey Hepburn

Here is what I have learned and share with others.

I taught singing, film acting and image classes on weekends for eight years at John Robert Powers School in San Jose, California.

I learned some valuable lessons myself through teaching.

Be mindful of what occupies your emotional body!

When acting on film where the actor's head on the big movie screen is as big as a table revealing their every emotion on their face, one can see what they are thinking vividly. When teaching acting and observing the students rehearse the same lines again and again and then performing for the camera for the final filming, the actor learns to perform as if it is the very first time they have ever heard the dialogue in the scene. They have to make it appear as real as if it is happening right now for the first time and react or respond to make it believable.

You and I have our favorite actors because they deliver a great, convincing performance and live the scene. The actor has to make a choice to either react or respond in order to be authentic in the scene. In life, it is best if we only react when it is an emergency or a surprise. People who react right away in most situations are lacking adequate control of their emotions.

A response is when one stops to think about what they want to say or do before they act on it. What does this have to do with inner beauty? A lot... when you have control over your emotions and you don't allow others to control you, life is good, and one's Inner Beauty can be most freely and sincerely expressed.

For instance, if someone asks you a question or requests that you do something for him or her and you are not sure if you can or how you feel about it... it's fine to say, "Let me think about it; I promise I will get back to you", or ..."Hmm, let me sleep on it, I will let you know".

Unless it is an emergency, you can take the time you need because no one has the right to make you answer or respond unless you choose to. You don't have to give an answer unless you can be sure it is the right answer for you and the situation. This helps a lot in dating, marriage, family and your work environment as well.

And perhaps most importantly, the biggest enemies we have are fear, self-consciousness and feeling sorry for ourselves. Life is too short.

Many people live in fear and don't even know it. It filters everything we do and say. Fear is the tenant in the basement of our body, temple or house and rules the rest of the rooms in a figurative sense. Just as the brain connects to all parts of our bodies, fear can work through you unnoticed, you accept how you feel, thinking, "This is just the way I am..." Many have said, "I can't help it." But I am here to tell you: Yes you can.

The tenants of fear are anger, guilt, shame, worry, anxiety, doubt, self-sabotage and I am sure you can think of one or two more.

In order to truly allow perceivable expression of our Inner Beauty, we have to evict fear and move in new feelings. It is impossible to be an empty shell.

We have to replace the negativity with positive, loving thoughts. Our negative thoughts have to be taken captive and replaced.

Have you ever been taking a shower and thinking thoughts about a potentially harmful situation and random thoughts come in that are something you would never say out loud to the person you are upset with ...but there you are, finding yourself in a scene, in reality, saying the very thing you thought would never come out of your mouth... you just blurt it out with no control? Trust me, if you think the same thought enough times you will eventually say it - and believe it.

At the risk of sounding a bit "scientific" about my approach to conveying the importance of including this chapter, I'll reference a quote from one of the history's most notable and influential people in reference to his belief system and how "cause and effect" play out in our everyday lives:

"Anyone who becomes seriously involved in the pursuit of science becomes convinced that there is a spirit manifest in the laws of the universe... a spirit vastly superior to that of man"
- Albert Einstein

Only God can renew your mind. All the positive thinking on your own is still making you the God of your own heart, mind, and soul.

When negative thoughts come in, take them captive and throw them out by replacing them with a loving thought, a forgiving thought. Think and recall the foundation of "Inner Beauty".

Did you know that to have compassion for another person is as simple as being kind?

Our brains create new baby neurons every morning and it's the time to pray, plan and be grateful, no matter what your circumstances are, it could always be worse.

We have to learn from our mistakes and be careful not to judge others. If we do judge others we may find ourselves in the same exact situation five or ten years from now.

It's ok to witness and see things in order to help a situation and to pray, but having the habit of judging people unless you get paid for it like Judge Judy can be a tricky thing.

Inner beauty has qualities that shine a light with a tranquil countenance.

Someone who has mastered the expression of their inner beauty has no jealousy and can promote a desire from others who want to be around them because they feel acknowledged and appreciated.

To be filled with inner beauty means to move and act in love, peace, patience, kindness, forbearance, perseverance, forgiveness and mercy.

There will be moments and sometimes hours or days when stress and the actions of others will affect you deeply.

There may be people who take unjustified advantage of your kindness and project their negative or guilty feelings towards you to make you feel bad. This too shall pass. You can forgive and make an executive decision to stay away from people who hurt your feelings.

The only real things that change in life under our own power are the people we associate with and the books we read.

In a nutshell, it's all about who you know and what you know.

There will also be times of loss and grieving. Loss of loved ones is natural and it seems when someone you love passes away, it brings up sad feelings of those you love that have passed on, left or abandoned you.

Although it may be difficult, try to stay grateful for the good memories and the time you had with them.

Remember that gratefulness and fear cannot co-exist. You are either living in one or the other.

Let your light shine from within you; let your love glow from your heart and through your eyes and rejoice in the expression and perfection of your own

Inner Beauty. You will see the world with a different perspective.

Keep your eyes and thoughts lifted upwards with hope and faith that things will work out even when they look like they might not.

Every day is a new day. Do what you can to help someone, find your purpose and make a difference in someone's life. It will help make a difference in yours.

Be sure to ask God for his guidance and your angels to protect you. Be blessed and dazzle the people around you with love and gratitude.

"Gratitude is the memory of the heart."
- Jean Baptiste Massieu

Mind is the Master

The word beauty is defined in the Merriam Webster's dictionary as: the quality or aggregate of qualities in a person or thing that gives pleasure to the senses or pleasurably exalts the mind or spirit.

A beautiful thinking person is humble and gracious. They are respectful and treat other people with kindness and respect, even if some of those people don't always deserve it. They have patience and are tactful, considerate and sensitive, helpful in any circumstance. They are also generous with their time, money or both when a dire need arises. They can graciously take a compliment as well as criticism. They are always grateful.

Integrity is all about being honest, about who you are, inside and out, and what choices you intend to make. Will you be trustworthy? Will you be pure in heart, thoughts, and actions?

It has come to my attention that people of accomplishment rarely sit back and let things happen to them. They go out and make things happen.

Some of the greatest secrets are hidden in plain sight. I learned from a very young age that words have power.

It happened after reading a poem in a book titled "As a Man Thinketh" by James Allen. It is written in old English text as follows:

Mind is the Master power
that moulds and makes,
And Man is Mind, and
evermore he takes,
The tool of Thought,
shaping what he wills,
Brings forth a thousand joys,
a thousand ills:
He thinks in secret,
and it comes to pass:
Environment is but
his looking glass.

It is more suggestive rather than explanatory, its objective is to stimulate people to the discovery and perception of the truth that -

"They themselves are makers of themselves."

We are always the master of our minds even in a weak and most abandoned state, but in weakness, we may become the foolish master who misgoverns our "household."

> "So you will be what you will to be;
> Let failure find its false content
> In that poor word, 'environment,'
> But spirit scorns it, and is free.
>
> "It masters time, it conquers space;
> It cowes that boastful trickster, Chance,
> And bids the tyrant Circumstance
> Uncrown, and fill a servant's place.
>
> "The human Will, that force unseen,
> The offspring of a deathless Soul,

Can hew a way to any goal,
Though walls of granite intervene.

"Be not impatient in delays
But wait as one who understands;
When spirit rises and commands
The gods are ready to obey."

The dreamers are the saviors of the world. Humanity cannot forget its dreamers; it cannot let their ideals fade and die; it lives in them; it knows them as the realities which it shall one day see and know.

Composer, sculptor, painter, poet, prophet and innovators, these are the architects of heaven. The world is beautiful because they have lived; without them, laboring humanity would perish.

You, who cherish a beautiful vision or a dream in your heart, will one day realize it. Cherish your visions; cherish your ideals; cherish the music that stirs in your heart, the beauty that forms in your mind and drapes your purest thoughts, for out of them will grow all delightful conditions, if you remain true to them, your world will, at last, be built.

To desire is to obtain; to aspire is to achieve, ask and you shall receive."

Dream magnificent dreams, and as you dream, you are building them. Your vision is the promise of what you shall one day realize.

I remember taking the bus one day as a teenager; I sat next to an elderly woman all dressed up with gloves and hat like she stepped out of a magazine. I couldn't help but compliment her and ask her a curious question, as she was so much older than I was, I wanted to know if she had wisdom to share with me.

I asked her if there was anything she would do differently if she had the chance to live her life again. She said, "Well, I would dream of the things I wanted and would like to do with my life or career. I would visualize the kind of man I would want to be with and someday marry. I would write it all down and then plant those seeds of thought in my heart and think about it every day. Every time I would think of it, it would be like watering the seeds of hope in my heart and then one day grow into the life I wanted.

I took her wisdom and planted it in my heart to write books and songs and create art in my life and I have and will continue.

What are your dreams?

Take some time and write them down, get a journal or write notes on your iPhone or smartphone and think of them often.

Take into consideration that the greatest achievements were at first and for a time just a dream. Dreams are the seedlings of realities.

Take for instance a youth who lives in a place with very little to offer, confined to long hours in an unhealthy workplace. But he dreams of better things, he thinks of how great it would be to have more intelligence and refinement someday. He spends his spare time developing his talents.

Years later we see this youth as a full-grown adult. In his hands, he runs a gigantic company and when he speaks, many lives are changed. He has realized the vision of his youth.

And you, too, will realize the vision of your heart, be it base or beautiful, or a mixture of both, for you will always gravitate toward that which you, secretly most love. Into your hands will be placed the exact results of your own thoughts; you will receive that which you earn; no more, no less.

Look at these successful people in the world: For instance, Walt Disney was told he lacked imagination. Believe it or not, the man who created many stories, an epic empire, and worldwide theme parks was once considered to not have much imagination.

During school, Thomas Edison had trouble learning in a traditional way and his teachers even told him that he was "too stupid to learn anything". Later, he was fired from his first two jobs for being too "unproductive". Despite his difficulties and failures, Thomas never stopped fighting for his dream.

Growing up, Michael Jordan was viewed as the 'goofy' kid who liked basketball. He wasn't very tall and didn't come from an athletic family. But he was determined. Michael had many setbacks and failures but his hard work eventually paid off.

We all know Steven Spielberg as one of the most famous filmmakers in history. But did you ever consider how he got to be where he is? Steven was highly determined and knew what he wanted from a young age. So, he took every opportunity he could to grow as a filmmaker and gain valuable knowledge from others. Can you believe that he even snuck into a filming of a real movie at the age of seventeen while on a tour at Universal Studios? After that, he spent his summers meeting directors, writers, and editors and learning from every conversation he had.

When J. K. Rowling first wrote Harry Potter, she was living as a single mother on welfare. It was a difficult life for her, but she decided to start writing. Now, look at her success.

Whatever your present environment may be, you will fall, remain, or rise with your thoughts and your vision.

You may be driving in your car, studying in a coffee shop or at home getting out of the shower as your mind wanders. Great ideas come to you, write them down. You may be practicing martial arts under the guidance of a master. And after a time he shall say, 'I have nothing more to teach you." And now you have become the master".

There is nothing you cannot achieve if the desire is in your heart and mind.

The thoughtless, the ignorant, and the lazy seeing only the apparent effects of things and not the things themselves, talk of luck, of fortune, and chance. Seeing someone grow rich, they say, "How lucky they are!" Observing another become intellectual, they exclaim, "How highly fortunate he is!"

They do not see the trials and failures and struggles, which these people most likely have encountered in order to gain wisdom and experience.

We may have no knowledge of the sacrifices they have made, or the fearless efforts they have made it through. We do not know the darkness and heartaches;

we only see the success and joy, and call it "luck".

In all human affairs, there are efforts and there are results, and the strength of the effort is the measure of the result.

The vision that you glorify in your mind, the ideal that you hold dear to your heart my friend, this you will build your life by, this you will one day become. You must never give up.

As for dark moments in life, take the time you need to grieve, gently give yourself permission to go through the stages of denial, anger, bargaining, depression, and acceptance, and when you accept your sorrow it can turn to peace...
- *Tricia Greenwood*

Worry Comes From Fear

Worry is lost energy. It is like a rocking chair that keeps going but never gets anywhere. It is a miserable habit. It makes you and others near you unhappy. Worry devastates your usefulness, injures your health and destroys your joy.

Worry can cause disease; dis-ease is a state of uneasiness.

A famous actress once said: "Worry is the foe of all beauty." She might have added: "It is the foe to all health."

I knew a successful businessman from Buffalo who said that his father worried for fifty-five years over an anticipated misfortune, which never arrived.

A clock would be of no use to keep time if it should become discouraged and come to a standstill by calculating its work a year ahead.

Life is like a mosaic, and each tiny piece must be cut and set with skill, first one piece, then another.

It is not the troubles of today, but those of tomorrow and next week and next year, that give us more wrinkles on our faces. It is all the fear of the unknown.

Mental exhaustion comes to those who look ahead, and climb mountains before reaching them.

Interesting enough to ponder, having faith is about believing in something you have not yet seen. It is faith that gives us hope.

Say to yourself... I am fearless. I am strong. I am free. I am successful. I am well. My faith is strong and shining within me. I shall be guided and protected by angels. I shall be given wisdom.

Boldly build a wall around today, and live within the enclosure. The past may have been hard, sad, or wrong, but it is over.

Why not turn it around? Instead of worrying over the unknown or the unexpected, set out with all your heart and soul to rejoice now in the unforeseen blessings of all your coming days.

What is this world we live in today, but as we see it? Create your own reality.

It's time to let go of selfish ambition. Make a change. Start something new, learn, discover, research and grow something in your life that was never there. Interesting people have a lot of interests. As you grow older you can add more interests and talents to your arsenal.

In order to achieve a joy-filled life free from the noise of society's online disrespect, envy, pettiness and all manner of negative attributes, we must understand the fact that we are entitled to a beautiful life free from all of that if we only acknowledge that as a reality and choose to access it now. Stay away from the chaos, you are in charge of what you see and hear.

Nothing changes in life until we do. Try laughing when you think you are going to cry. It's not so crazy and it really helps.

Everyone likes someone who can enjoy a laugh at their own expense, for it shows good humor and good sense. If you laugh at yourself, other people will not laugh at you. Well, hopefully. Choose your friends wisely... I say fondly with a wink.

Ten things are necessary for happiness in this life, the first being a good digestion, and the other nine are money. At least, it's what has been said and written by modern philosophers and money magazines.

He alone is the happy man who has learned to evoke happiness from the present conditions that surround him.

The person who has mastered the "secret" will not wait for ideal surroundings or wait until next year, next decade or until winning the lottery but will make the most out of life today, right now.

Paradise is here or nowhere, you must take your joy with you or you will never find it.

It has been known that it's after business hours, not in them, that people break down. When they go home and find unrest. We must turn the key on business when we leave it, and unlock the doors of some wholesome recreation or re-creation.

Re-creation comes in many forms, reading a good book, painting, gardening, and a nap in a hammock under a tree, fishing, or rock climbing. We can get information in seconds on how to do something on YouTube or Netflix.

We have iPads, Kindles and cell phones to read eBooks. No matter where we are we can learn everything we want to know right at our fingertips, what could be better? Playing online games is fun too.

"It is a grand thing to live, to open our eyes in the morning and look out upon the world, and enjoy the sunshine, it is a good thing simply to be alive. Life is short.

"One ought, every day," says Goethe, "at least to hear a little song, read a good poem, see a fine picture, and, if it were possible, to speak a few reasonable words." And if this be good for one's self, why not try the song, the poem, the picture, and the good words, on someone else?

One who has intellectual resources to fall back upon will not lack for wholesome daily recreation.

"He is the happiest," said by Goethe, "be he king or peasant, who finds peace in his home."

"Pleasant words are sweet to the soul and give health to our bodies." It's the negative fault finding insinuations, sharp sarcastic criticisms and unkind words that create most of the division and unhappiness in couples, families, and co-workers.

There are too many serious-minded fathers and mothers who do not take the time to play with their children or who are known to their neighbors as "the happy family."

In the Bible it is said, "provoke not your children to wrath," it means literally, "do not irritate your children;" "do not rub them the wrong way."

Children should never get the impression that they live in a hopeless, cold world; they learn what they live. It is up to the adults in the family to create a household of cheerfulness, to help transform their children's lives like sunlight, making their hearts glad about little things, rejoicing upon small fun experiences and special occasions.

"To love, and to be loved," is the greatest happiness in the world.
- *Sydney Smith*

"How beautiful would a child's home life be if at bed time they would say, "We've had such a wonderful day today!'"

Children should be taught the habit of finding pleasure everywhere and to see the bright side of everything. It can be taught and learned.

We ought to have teachers who are able to educate and inspire our children in this department of their natures quite as much as in music or art.

Think about it, you or I cannot become an accomplished scientist in a few weeks or months, not even in a few years. But only after many years of focused study could we speak with authority in a given field or career.

Likewise, you or I cannot acquire self-control, and have the wisdom and peace giving knowledge, which self-control establishes, but by patient interest and study that runs silently within, until there comes a time where it has been attained. Introspection of self is when the mental eye is turned like a searchlight upon the inner things of the mind where its subtle processes are observed and carefully emphasized. It's a matter of stepping aside from selfish gratifications and excitements of worldly pleasures in order to observe, with the objective of understanding one's own nature. This is the beginning of self-control.

Self-analysis is taking the time to observe the tendencies of the mind; they are then closely examined, and are put through a rigid process of analysis. The negative tendencies are (those that produce painful effects) they are separated from the good tendencies (those that produce peaceful effects); taking note of the particular actions they produce in our personality.

Understanding the results that spring from these actions are then grasped, enabling us to follow them in their profound consequences. It is a process of testing and proving. Keep a journal.

By this time, the practical student of things divine has clearly before them every tendency and aspect of their nature, and the suggestions of the mind and subtle motives of the heart. There is not a spot or corner left, which has not been explored with the light of self-examination.

It is considered the height of wisdom to be able to see ourselves as others see us, but the practitioner of self-control goes far beyond this: we not only see ourselves as others see us, *we see ourselves as we are.*

We are no longer in a state of confusion, but have gained a glimpse of the laws, which operate in the world of thought, and can now begin to adjust our mind in accordance with those laws.

When we stand face to face with our real inner self, not trying to hide away from any secret fault, we see the full magnitude of the task, which lies before us.

There is a process of weeding, sifting, and cleansing. As the farmer cleans and prepares the ground for his crops, so the student must remove the weeds of negativity from their mind; cleansing and purifying the mind to sow the seeds of righteous actions, which will in turn produce the harvest of a consistent good life.

Instead of thinking and acting blindly, when our nature is stimulated or our buttons are pushed, we can now decide and choose our thoughts and deeds.

We are no longer a slave of our human nature and circumstances; you and I become the master of our own nature and circumstances. We are no longer carried here and there on the impulsive forces of our reactions because we can control and guide these forces to the realization of our own positive and rightful purpose.

When you have your nature in control and refuse to think thoughts of doing deeds, which oppose the righteous law, you will rise above the dominion of sin and sorrow, you will rise above ignorance and doubt, and become strong, calm, and peaceful.

Our worst enemies are not outside of us, but inside of us. Every human being harbors a traitor who is always on the watch to thwart his ambition, to turn him aside from his aim. That traitor is called Doubt.

You must make up your mind at the very beginning of your endeavor, career or your new school year that you will always be somewhat attacked by certain mental enemies, mental traitors, which will try to dissuade you from doing the highest or biggest thing possible that you try to accomplish.

The person who is not strong enough to resist its deceitful attacks, will never do what they are capable of doing, and were sent into this world by the Creator to do.

Doubt makes us afraid to start out on a course we desire to achieve our goals. Our dreams we ought to pursue more than any other thing, because doubt will be standing right at the gateway of the choices and plans we have made. Right when we have decided to take the path that is best for achieving that goal or dream, that's when doubt calls a halt.

Doubt causes us to pause and think again, tells us no one really cares if we achieve this or that anyway, and asks us to look again at the rugged path we have chosen and to consider whether we really want to pay the price of what it will take to accomplish our goals and dreams. You have to destroy that mean voice of Doubt.

At the very outset of your career make up your mind that you are going to be a conqueror in life, that you are going to be the king or queen of your mental realm and not a slave to any treacherous mental enemy and that you will choose the wisest course, no matter how difficult.

Don't let doubt destroy your efforts. Don't let it paralyze you because you have a waiting giant within you. Be filled with courage and self-confidence; it will kill the giant traitor named Doubt.

To overcome doubt and have self-respect and self-esteem you must have a personal value system based on morality. It's important to value yourself, and to value others.

I believe the price tag you put on yourself is what others will value you at. It may sound materialistic but is only a simile, to help measure your opinion of yourself.

How you value yourself includes your purpose in life, your potential, your job, achievements and ability to stand on your own. Get these things in order in your life. Someone with a good self-esteem and confidence likes to meet new people and doesn't worry about being judged by them. They are able to learn and grow from their mistakes instead of beating themselves up over and over again. You have to love yourself, not in a narcissistic way, but you have to love yourself and be kind to yourself. All the experiences and people in your life have either added or taken away from you, only you can control what you keep in life and what you leave behind.

By perfecting ourselves in self-esteem and self-control we acquire divine knowledge. By having mastered the science of self-control we will bring order out of confusion.

The empowering knowledge of self, which includes our behavior, character, intuition and intelligence are framed upon the same law of love. Gaining divine peace and knowledge is in essence the desire to understand others and be understood in order to enhance one's life and create wonderful relationships.

Wisdom is the ability to apply knowledge and experience, understanding or insight to any given situation or plan. It may be said of those who have never worked on their own nature to control and purify it, that they cannot clearly discern between good and evil or right and wrong. There seems to be shades of gray and confusion in their lives.

They reach after things which they think will give them pleasure, and try to avoid those things which they believe might cause them pain, and sometimes find themselves in situations they did not see coming.

The source of their actions is self, and they only discover what is right by painful experiences that have caused heartbreak, depression, and suffering. But one who practices self-control gains the knowledge, which enables them to act from the moral law, which sustains the universe.

Knowing good and evil, right and wrong enables us to live in accordance with good and right. Deception is a very silent yet powerful spirit, that causes us to see things not as they are. The more real and honest you are, the more you will be able to see through people and know if what and who they are is real. You will see through manipulative and fake people and walk away from them.

Grief, anxiety, and fear are the enemies of our soul in human life. We should fight against every influence which tends to depress the mind, as we would against a temptation to crime. It is beyond question that the mind has the power to lengthen our youthfulness and beauty.

The lover of peace enters a room and lights it up with every step. The first step towards the heights of wisdom and peace is to understand the darkness and real misery of selfishness. When it is truly understood, the overcoming of it, the coming out of it will soon follow.

Selfishness not only exists in greed and uncontrolled conditions of the mind, it's in every hidden thought connected with the assumption and glorification of one's self. It is most deceiving and subtle when it prompts us to dwell upon the selfishness in others, to accuse them of it and to talk about it. The person who continually dwells upon the selfishness in others will not overcome their own selfishness. It's not by accusing others that we come out of negativity and selfish thoughts, but by purifying our own minds and cleansing ourselves.

Telling the same brash stories about past hurts or your ex's head trips, or current sweethearts' ex's lies and betrayals to anyone who will listen is unproductive. They only serve to hurt, and are negative and useless.

Rehearsing the same old stories will only re-open your old wounds and make the scars even deeper every time you tell them. Stop doing it! Don't re-tell hurtful experiences to anyone, especially a new friend or an acquaintance in order to bond with them in misery. It doesn't achieve anything and these types of thoughts are obviously not exercising new thoughts with Beautiful Thinking

Have the courage to forgive others who have caused you to have negative memories. I know it may be hard to forgive some of them. The solution is to pray for them. It will help you to forgive them for their ignorance or mean selfishness.

It's important for us to think in a more compassionate way, if their sickly actions and thoughts caused you pain, guilt or shame; the way to cleanse yourself from it is to do just that. Cleanse yourself, release it from your heart, mind, and soul, erase the incident or terrible experience and let it go. Release yourself from the prison of their doing.

No one has the power to make you feel less than you choose. We have free will, it is the most powerful force within you. Only God can supernaturally renew your mind. But we have to ask him in prayer and petition. Write it down, all your feelings. Let the cleansing begin.

By patiently overcoming our own desire to hold on to the wrongs done to us, we ascend into freedom. Only when we have conquered ourselves are we able to conquer others' attempts to steal our peace; not by anger, but by love.

The way from anger to peace is not found in the outer world of people; it is in the inner world of thoughts. It does not consist in altering the actions of others; it consists in perfecting our own actions and our own thoughts. It is in the practice of Beautiful Thinking.

Charlie Jones said, "You will be the same person in five years as you are today except for the people you meet and the books you read."

Making Mistakes

It's not a good idea to punish or criticize yourself for mistakes you yourself have made. You're not alone; everyone has made mistakes and has hurt others.

Everyone has had issues and met trouble and misfortune. It is by undergoing trials like these that we gain experience and wisdom. Sometimes a misunderstanding will lead to a deeper conversation that eventually creates a deeper bond between two people. We are enabled to correct our future actions by applying the lessons, which our mistakes have taught us.

Yesterday is dead; forget it. Live today, stay busy, be determined on doing what's right and accomplishing things in your life that are worthwhile.

Looking at my life experiences, I think of the past memories as if they are like fruit on a tree. There is some bad fruit and good fruit, I just throw away all the bad fruit and eliminate it from my heart and mind, and so can you. Take the time to pray and meditate, forgive yourself of all your mistakes. Forgive others for theirs.

Maybe there is a relationship with a relative that was unhealthy and stressed you out, and you have stayed away from them because you feel verbally or emotionally abused. You have the right to stay away from them for your own emotional health.

Perhaps there was an incident with a friend or relative that caused your relationship to fall apart due to circumstances beyond your control and you wish you could be close again.

The best way I know to re-establish the relationship is to give them a gift in secret. What I mean is, don't wait for a holiday or a reason to give a gift, go out today and buy a gift and a card with an apology.

Send it with no expectation of a response.

This may be hard... but if you have self-control, you will understand that you cannot control others.

By not having an expectation of an immediate response and having more patience for this person, you will know in your heart that you have done a right thing.

It may take some time for them to respond. It may be that they never do, but their memory of you will be a better one than what it would have been if you had not taken the action and followed through to show your love and kindness.

I was in a church service where the Pastor told a person at the beginning of the first row a statement, it was then repeated in the ear of each person in the same row until it got to the last person who was to stand up and recite what they heard. It was amusing because it was nothing like the original statement. You will meet people who like to talk more about others than themselves because it distracts them from their own problems.

If you learn someone is talking negatively about you, don't worry, it will soon blow over. Today's papers end up in the trash. Tomorrow the world will soon forget. Let go… and let God take your hurt feelings and heal them.

Just know that on this earth, kindness and love are investments, which bring us more happiness today. Believe this my friend and say it to yourself: "If I live today in accordance with what I sincerely believe is in tune with God's purpose for my life, I shall in my future benefit by these acts."

Everything lives and dies in accordance with the plan of the creator of the universe. You and I are atoms in the universe, which is governed by a power too big and too great for us to comprehend.

The sun goes down behind the skyline in the West as it has done for millions and millions of years. I sit and meditate on the big picture at times looking at the sunset with a deeper appreciation of God and a profound faith in his wisdom and works.

I have gone down many paths through the years and met many unique individuals. I have studied many rules of thought. My conclusion is; we are not alone.

God rules and plans. Let us strive to be appreciative of Him and understand that failure is impossible to us if we keep on doing the best we can.

By speaking softly, showing kindness today to as many people we come in contact with, and living in accordance to a generous and compassionate plan for our lives, we will be at peace no matter what the circumstances.

The two most powerful warriors are patience and time.
- Leo Tolstoy

Anger

Anger and revenge can be great enemies to our health. Anger makes blood rush to our head, weakens our body, and distorts our vision.

Anger can give us nervous conditions, weak stomachs and poor judgment. We might lose friends or be driven to despair and addictions. When we are older, anger and resentment will likely lead to a stroke.

When two men have differences, watch the cool man finish victoriously and the angry man always loses. Keep your head; let the other person fret and fume. He will tie himself up in a knot, and be the loser.

Serenity is one of God's blessings to cherish. Fortunate is the man or woman who can hold their serenity.

When you get a letter that stirs you to anger, don't answer that letter right away, wait for at least forty-eight hours, then write a moderately bitter letter and then tear it up.

I know you are tempted and upset, and your limit of endurance is sometimes reached. But I also know that revenge is sweet only in anticipation. I know that revenge by anger and by the cruel "eye for an eye" measure is never sweet or right.

Being the victim of imposition, ingratitude and being falsely accused is so hard to deal with. Dealing with accusations that you are completely innocent of has got to be one of the worst feelings to experience in life. Especially when you cannot defend yourself and it seems like there is nothing you can say that will make them believe your innocence. The way from anger to peace is not by projecting painful blame against others, but by overcoming one's self. The thing that works for me when I have been caught in a state of confusion and upset over a matter is to write down whatever is on my mind about that person or situation. Be it a family situation, a love interest, a work-related issue or any type of relationship.

I get all my feelings out on paper and I find it makes me cry sometimes as I am writing which helps me to release any hurt or anger. Then I read it out loud and ask God to take these feelings away from me. I then tear it up into little pieces and burn it on a cookie sheet outside by where I find a place to bury it in the ground. I know it sounds strange, but it works. I pray again to have forgiveness for the person and myself to be filled with love and light from above.

All I can advise it that time and prayer will someday bring out the truth. Not to be vindictive, but to know that sooner or later all will come to know the truth.

A forgiving attitude and self-respect will give you the strength you need to take charge of your thoughts and words. You can overcome your past hurt and issues with others without the fear of rejection.

No one can make you feel like a victim of circumstance but you. Be strong and do the opposite of what your human nature might dictate. It's hard but the outcome will strengthen your relationships and your character.

Holding grudges will only harm you. I'm sure you have heard the saying that having unforgiveness within you for someone is like drinking poison yourself and waiting for the other person to die.

I have an analogy that deals with this type of calm needed. Picture a pond of cool clear water and you want to stop and take a drink. All of a sudden a herd of wild animals run through it and all the dirt from the bottom rises to the surface. If you will just wait for a little while, the water will eventually become clear again and the truth will be known, then you can drink the cool clear water and quench your thirst. Patience is a virtue we all need.

The Storm of Depression

There are thousands of people who have lost everything most valued to them in this world from war, divorce, fires and other natural or man-made disasters. All the material results of their lives' endeavor, and yet, because they possess stout hearts, unconquerable spirits, and a determination to push ahead which knows no retreat, they are just as far from real failure as before their loss; and with such invulnerable wealth, they can never be "poor".

A great many people fail to reach a success that matches their ability because they are victims of their moods, which repels people and business. Everywhere we see people with great ambitions doing very ordinary things, simply because there are so many days when they do not "feel like it" or when they are discouraged or "blue." It is perfectly possible for a well-trained mind to completely route out the worst case of the "blues" in a few minutes;

but the trouble with most of us is that instead of flinging open the mental blinds and letting in the sun of cheerfulness, hope, and optimism, we keep them closed and try to eject the darkness from within, without the light we need.

The art of arts is learning how to clear your mind of its enemies. Did you know that when the Bible speaks of our enemies in the Psalms, it is literally our thoughts. We have enemies of our comfort, happiness, and success. It is a great thing to learn to focus our mind upon the beautiful things in life instead of the ugly, the true instead of the false, upon harmony instead of discord, of life instead of death, health instead of disease.

This is not always easy, but it is possible and available to everybody. It requires only skillful thinking, the forming of the right thought habits. The best way to keep out darkness is to keep one's life filled with light; to keep out discord, keep it filled with harmony; to shut out error, keep your mind filled with truth; to shut out ugliness, contemplate beauty and loveliness; to get rid of all that is sour and unwholesome, contemplate all that is sweet and wholesome. Opposite thoughts cannot occupy the mind at the same time.

No matter whether you "feel like it" or not, simply affirm that you *must* feel like it, that you *will* feel like it, that you *do* feel like it, that you are normal and that you are in a position to do your best. Say it *deliberately, affirm it vigorously* and it *will* come true.

Constant discouragements are a great temptation to abandon your life dreams and to drop your standards. This is because our very first discouraging moments in life occur during the most formative segment of our development.

Our vision is apt to become blurred in passing through great crises, in periods of general depression and in times of financial stress, but this is really the test of character. He who does not allow obstacles to divert him from his one aim, who is made of the stuff that wins, hangs on to his vision, even to the point of starvation, knows that there is only one way of bringing it down to earth, and that is by clinging to it through storm and stress, in spite of every obstacle and discouragement.

It seems most people at one time or another in their lives have wished they would just disappear or asked God for them not to ever wake. Some think about ending their lives because the world and some people become too much to take. I have asked for God to take me after my only son passed away. Now, I have faith my spirit will recognize his in heaven.

There are times in life when relationships don't work out no matter how hard we try. Believing that fate supersedes dominion over our thoughts is to believe that we are helpless to change our circumstances. When one door closes, another one opens.

You never know what is down the road or around the corner. There are no coincidences in life. When things go wrong, don't say why me?

Think these words to yourself, "There must be something valuable I am going to learn from this situation or I will gain more wisdom from this experience."

Many notable motivational speakers have attested to the fact that something so simple as "changing their thinking" renders that old adage to actually read, "Whenever one door closes, two more open!" This alone, will cause us to *embrace* rather than *dread* the closing of doors along our chosen path.

Gloom and depression not only take much out of our life, but also detract greatly from the chances of winning success. It is the bright and cheerful spirit that wins the final triumph. Never mind what failures, discouragements or misfortunes "come to you". Let no one person, or combinations of unfortunate circumstances destroy your faith in the ability to achieve even the "loftiest of goals".

Your dream of what you believe you were born to do is a dream for the purpose of guidance toward the eventual reality. Never mind how the actual facts may seem to contradict the results you are after. No matter who may oppose you or how much others may attempt to advise or condemn your attempt, cling to your vision, because it is sacred.

It is the God-urge in you. You have no right to allow it to fade or to become dim. Your final success will be measured by your ability to cling to your vision through any discouragement. It will depend largely upon your stick-to-it-tive-ness; your bulldog tenacity. If you shrink before criticism and opposition you will demagnetize your mind and lose all the momentum, which you have previously gained in your endeavors. No matter how dark or threatening the outlook, keep working, keep visualizing your dreams and goals, and some unexpected way will surely open for its fulfillment.

The next time you get into trouble, or are discouraged and find yourself giving in to thoughts that attempt to persuade you to believe that you are a failure, just try the experiment of affirming persistently, that all that is real must be good, for God made all that is, and whatever doesn't seem to be good is not like its creator and therefore cannot be real. You will be surprised to see how unfortunate suggestions and adverse conditions will melt away before it.

The next time you get discouraged and feel the "blues" or a spell of depression coming on, just take a good long bath or a long shower and dress yourself in your best outfit and go out for your favorite dessert. Give yourself a good talking to in the same dead-in-earnest way that you would talk to your own child or a dear friend who was deep in depression or melancholy. Drive out the dark thoughts, the hideous pictures that haunt your mind. Sweep away all depressing thoughts, suggestions, and all the rubbish that is troubling you. Let go of everything that is unpleasant; all the mistakes, all the disagreeable past; just rise up in arms against the enemies of your peace and happiness. Summon all the force and willpower you can muster within yourself and drive them out. Resolve that no matter what happens you are going to be happy; that you are going to enjoy yourself and you are going to succeed in all your endeavors.

Put out of your mind forever any thought that you could possibly fail in reaching the goal of your longing. Set your face toward it; keep looking steadfastly in the direction of your ambition, whatever it may be; resolve never to recognize defeat, and you will by your mental attitude create a tremendous force of your own to lift you up and out of the mind-space that is adversarial to your best interests.
If you have the grit and will power to

persevere to the end, if you persistently maintain the victorious attitude toward your vision, victory will crown your efforts.

Have courage to go on and be brave. You have power over your emotions. Give yourself permission to exercise that power. Make an executive decision regarding your feelings and choose how you want to feel about it and how you are going to deal with the situation. Let no one tell you how you should feel or be.

My hope is that if you know someone dealing with depression or has been through a horrific life experience, you will get this book for them to read or visit them and read a chapter to them.

My friend, Matthew Dovel, is the author of a book titled "My Last Breath". He is a Behavioral Scientist and the President of international suicide prevention nonprofit. Supportisp.org

Matthew says: "Education has been shown

to be the best method for reducing suicide rates. By understanding the psychology of the suicidal thought process, we can better understand how to approach it, and for most, this is a temporary state of mind.

In order to reduce and/or eliminate suicidal thoughts the individual having these thoughts must be able to communicate with others that they are having them. The fact is, having suicidal thoughts are part of the human experience, and anyone given the right situation and/or circumstance can have them.

As we experience our journey through life we record everything in our mind in the form of memories. There are two types of memories: the experience itself and the emotional state we were having at the time of an experience. Our ability to recall any past memory is based on the intensity of our emotional state at the time of the experience. Life experiences are what we use to navigate through life teaching us how to respond to situations and circumstances for social, relational interaction, and basic survival skills.

According to scientific research, humans have only two core emotions: love, and fear. All emotions can be traced back to these two emotions. We are born with only two natural fears: loud noises and the fear of falling. All other fears are learned through experience or conditioning. Learned fears can be removed as easily as they are learned through the process of desensitizing.

Being very close to someone that we love and having one of these examples happen: like a "Dear John" letter, a temporary separation, divorce, or death of a loved one or that of a close friend can really hurt.

Did you know our diets play a large part in our ability to face difficult life issues and new experiences that can be life-changing events. It is recommended that to be mentally alert, physically strong, and emotionally sound, one should, whenever possible, avoid foods that contain toxins, sugars, antibiotics, growth hormones, GMOs (Genetically Modified Organisms), and cancer causing preservatives. Try to eat organically grown, natural whole foods.

Einstein once said, "Imagination is more powerful than knowledge," and he was right. Everything we do is preceded by an image in our mind! When we see positive experiences for our future, generally we will have positive results. If we see things going sideways and messed up, the results usually will live up to our expectations.

God gave us the power of choice, and we are the only creatures on this planet that do not live by pure instincts alone!

However, we still are driven by instinctual desires at times. We create and choose the images we see in our mind. If you are not in control of your mind, now is a good time to change that status, and this is how. Your brain will assume you are happy when you smile really big and release dopamine. Dopamine is a natural endorphin that our bodies create causing the sensation of pleasure, way more powerful than heroin without the cost or side effects.

Think of forty things that make your life worth living for, and then make a list of all positive experiences you can remember. Get a personal journal at the bookstore or online. Forty is a number to shoot for, so if you can only come up with five items to start don't worry about it. Your list will grow over time and maybe then it will be more or less than forty.

Gather as many big, positive, happy experiences you have had as you can, especially the ones that put a smile on your face when you think of them. Some examples are: ice cream, a first kiss, a vacation, a sunset, winning at something, the sound of rain on the roof, a really good meal, etc. This list is a lifelong project in a constant state of updating with new and exciting experiences.

Whenever you are feeling emotionally drained or depressed, pull out this list, and focus on one item at a time. Relive each item completely with all the sights, sounds, emotions, smells, and tastes. When you do this as instructed, you will release dopamine a natural endorphin stimulating the pleasure centers on the brain."

Matthew shares his story with those who are struggling with their lives and his near-death experience has helped thousands. He was on, "Good Morning America" and you can learn more about him on Youtube and the internet. I met Matthew Dovel when he invited me to perform my first album, "No Fear in Love" at a fundraiser he put on to help prevent suicide at the Henderson Pavilion in Henderson, Nevada.

Hold That Thought

Once you know what is right or the right thing to do, it's really hard <u>not</u> to do it.

When someone is talking to you about a particular subject and you have to stop them in the midst of it, the one way to get up and go do the thing you must, is to hold up your index finger and say to them "Hold that thought" and go do what you need to do. When you come back, ask them to continue on.

What might be important to you means nothing to others. Sometimes in life we don't get what we want. We get something else entirely.

One of the great dividing-lines in human life is the threshold-line. On one side of this line a person has their 'world within the world,' the sanctuary of love, the sheltered place of peace, the scene of life's most personal and exclusive obligations.

And on the other side lies the larger life of mankind wherein also a person must take their place and do their work. Life is spent in crossing this threshold-line, going out to the many and coming in to the few, going out to answer the call of labor and coming in to take the right to rest.

The constant struggle to measure up to a high ideal is the only force in heaven or on earth that can make a life great, beautiful and fruitful.

If we would ever accomplish anything of worth, if we would ever establish our oneness with the Creator, and accomplish the work He sent us here to do, we must live up to our ideal.

With eyes fixed on this ideal, we must work with a faith that never grows dim, with a patience that is akin to genius, we must persevere unto the end; for, as we advance, our ideal steadily moves upward.

It is only by daily patience and thought

and care that we can cease to be an obstruction to the best power for giving and receiving. At times we can be our own worst enemies.

In its simplest form, patience is a calm and unshaken state of mind, strongly bearing up against a present burden of distress.

With due respect to our own natural temperament of being human beings, some of us can naturally bear more than others. The degree of pain we bear is to be measured, not by the force of the blow, but the power of resistance.

That which would crush a reed shall leave no mark upon an oak. When pain comes, however, it is well if we have learned a natural means of enduring it. But practice, discipline, and exercise add vastly even to this natural fortitude.

Fresh soldiers and new recruits shrink and flee, but the veteran has looked death in the face. He, who has endured once, can endure again. Still more effective is the inward principle: by adding moral motives to one's insightful natural power.

Though pains of mind may be worse than pains in the body, someone with much tranquility may also endure them, for this we call fortitude, in some circumstances, we call it long suffering with immeasurable patience.

By great skill and self-control in managing our thoughts and detaching the attention from distressing objects, some of us are able, to a degree which at first might seem most impracticable, to keep up quietude and even a humble show of cheerfulness.

Scientific Thoughts on Worry

Dr. George W. Jacoby was known as one of the foremost American brain doctors in the world.

In regard to "the investigations of the neurologists," he said, "it's no secret, in recent years, the discovery that worry has killed more people in the last century than have been killed in battle".

This is the final, up-to-date word. "Not only is it known," resumes the great neurologist, counting off his words, as it were, on his finger-tips, "that worry kills, but the most minute details of its murderous methods are familiar to modern scientists".

It is a common belief of those who have made a special study of the science of brain diseases that hundreds of deaths attributed to other causes each year are due simply to worry. In plain English, worry works its irreparable injury through certain cells of our brains.

These harmful inroads upon the system can be best likened to the constant falling of drops of water in one spot. In the brain it is the insistent, never-lost idea, the single, constant thought, centered upon one subject, which in the course of time destroys the brain cells.

The healthy brain can cope with day-to-day occasional worry; it is the iteration and reiteration of disquieting thoughts that the cells of the brain cannot successfully combat.

"The mechanical effect of worry is much the same as if the skull were laid bare and the brain exposed to the action of a little hammer beating continually upon it day after day, until the membranes are disintegrated and the normal functions disabled.

It's the maddening thought that will not be crushed, the haunting, ever-present idea that is not or cannot be rid of by our own doing, is the theoretical hammer which diminishes the vitality of the sensitive nerve organisms, the minuteness of which makes the activity of the neural circuits visible to the eye only under a very powerful 3D microscope that lets doctors see inside the brain.

The cells are intimately connected, joined together by little fibers, and they in turn are in close relationship with the cells of the other parts of the brain. These connections in the brain are called dendrites that store all the information. The dendrites look like branches of trees. There is much to understand in how our brain works. I highly advise you looking into it and you can learn more from the book, "Switch on My Brain" by Dr. Carolyn Leaf. I also have the audiobook to listen to while I drive.

"Worry is itself a species of monomania. Where your mind is restricted to the same thought over and over, no mental attitude is more disastrous to personal happiness, and personal usefulness in the world, than worry and its twin, despondency. The remedy for this evil lies in training the will to cast off these thoughts and seek a change of occupation, when the first warning is sounded by nature causing depression. Relaxation is the certain foe of worry, and 'don't fret' one of the healthiest of mottos."

In a life of constant worrying, we are as much behind the times as if we were to go back to use the first steam engines that wasted ninety percent of the energy of the coal, instead of having an electric dynamo that utilizes ninety per cent of the power.

Some people waste a large percentage of their energy in fretting and worry, and constantly complaining about the weather and the news they read and hear from different sources of fake media.

Others convert nearly all of their energy into power and moral sunshine. He who has learned the true art of living will not waste his energies in conflict, which accomplishes nothing, but merely grinds out the machinery of life. Grief, anxiety, and fear are great enemies of human life.

A depressed, melancholy soul, a life that has ceased to believe in its own power, in its own mission has become crippled and useless. We should fight against every influence that tends to depress the mind, as we would against a temptation to crime. It is undoubtedly true that, as a rule, the mind has power to lengthen the period of youthful and mature strength and beauty.

Selfless Love

Love, Wisdom and Peace: this tranquil
state of mind and heart may be attained,
and realized by all who are willing and
ready to yield up self, and who are
prepared to humbly enter into an
understanding of all that the giving up of
self involves.

Some people are chained to thoughts and
feelings that causes much suffering
because they think their small dark prison
of self is all they have to hold on to, and
they are afraid that if they desert that
prison they will lose all that is real and
worth having.

We can choose to stop suffering. When
you understand that the indwelling power
that forged those chains and built the
dark and narrow prison, can break away
when it desires and wills to do so, and the
soul does will to do so when it has
discovered the worthlessness of its prison,

when long-suffering has prepared it for the reception of the boundless light and love. As the shadow follows the form, and as smoke comes after the fire, so effect follows cause, and suffering and bliss follow the thoughts and deeds of men.

People reap a harvest of suffering because in the near or distant past they have sown the seeds of evil; they reap a harvest of bliss also as a result of their own sowing of the seeds of good.

The world does not understand the love that is selfless because it is engrossed in the pursuit of its own pleasures, and cramped within the narrow limits of perishable interests, mistaking, in its ignorance, those pleasures and interests for real and abiding things.

Caught in the flames of fleshly lusts, and burning with anguish, it sees not the pure and peaceful beauty of truth. Feeding upon wrongdoing and self-delusion, it is shut out from the mansion of all-seeing love.

Not having this love, not understanding it, people inquire of outward transformations of engaging in rituals which involve no real inward sacrifice, and each imagines that their reform is going to right the world forever, while they continue to propagate evil by engaging it in their own heart.

Let the rich cease to despise the poor, and the poor cease to condemn the rich; let the greedy learn how to give, and the lustful how to grow pure; let the uncharitable begin to forgive; and the slanderers grow ashamed of their conduct. Therefore, whoever purifies his or her own heart is the world greatest benefactor.

Where hatred, dislike, and condemnation are, selfless love does not abide. It resides only in the heart that has ceased from all condemnation.

If you love people and speak of them with praise until they frustrate you in some way, or do something you resent, and then you dislike them and speak badly of them, the law of love does then not characterize you. If in your heart, you are continually convicting and condemning others, selfless love is hidden from you. Such are the people who are considered self-centered.

One who knows that love is at the heart of all things, and has realized the all-sufficing power of that love, has no room in his heart for condemnation.

One whose heart is centered in love does not brand others and does not seek to convert others to their own views, and try to convince them of the superiority of their beliefs and methods. When we know and understand the law of love and truth, we will live it and maintain a calm attitude of mind and sweetness of heart toward all.

Only the pure in heart see God, and when your heart is sufficiently purified you will enter into a new birth within, and the love of God that does not die, nor change, nor end in pain and sorrow will be awakened within you, and you will be at peace.

The person who strives for the attainment of divine love is ever seeking to overcome the spirit of condemnation, for where there is pure spiritual knowledge, condemnation cannot exist, and only in the heart that has become incapable of condemnation is love perfected and fully realized.

Train your mind in strong, impartial, and gentle thought; train your heart in purity and compassion; train your tongue to silence and to true and stainless speech; so shall you enter the way of holiness and peace.

So living, without seeking to convert, you will convince; without arguing, you will teach; not cherishing ambition, the wise will find you out; and without striving to gain men's opinions, you will subdue their hearts.

For love is all conquering, all-powerful;
and the thoughts, deeds, and words of
love can never perish.

To know that love is universal and
supreme; to be freed from the shackles of
evil; to know that all people are striving to
realize the truth each in their own way; to
be satisfied within and serene: this is
peace; this is the true realization of
selfless love.

"Musicians must make music, artists
must paint, poets must write if they are
ultimately to be at peace with themselves.
What humans can be, they must be."
- *Abraham Maslow*

Peace Within

Bring every thought, every impulse, and every desire into perfect obedience to the divine power within you. Come away for a while from external things, from the pleasures of the senses, from the arguments of the intellect, from the noise and the excitements of the world.

Silence your cell phone and walk away from your computer and television. Stop and take a walk into nature or go lie on your bed. Withdraw yourself into the innermost chamber of your heart, free from the immoral intrusion of all selfish desires, you will find a deep silence, a holy calm, and if you will rest awhile in that holy place and will meditate there, the faultless eye of truth will open within you, and you will see things as they really are.

This holy place within you is your real and eternal self; it is the divine within you; and only when you identify yourself with it can you be said to be "clothed and in your right mind." It is the abode of peace, the temple of wisdom, the dwelling-place of immortality.

Apart from this inward resting-place, there can be no true peace, no knowledge of the divine, and if you can remain there for one minute, one hour, or one day, it is possible for you to remain there always.

All your sins and sorrows, your fears and anxieties are your own, and you can cling to them or you can give them up. No one else can give up worry and sin for you; you must give it up yourself.

The greatest teacher can do no more than walking the way of truth for himself and then point it out to you. You must walk the way of truth for yourself.

You can obtain freedom and peace within by your own efforts, by yielding up that which binds the soul, and which is destructive of peace.

The angels of divine peace and joy are always at hand, and if you do not see them or hear them, it is because you shut yourself out from them, and entertain thoughts engaging in the company of the spirits of worry and anger within you.

You are what you will be, what you wish to be, what you prefer to be. You can if you are willing to commence to purify yourself, and arrive at peace, or you can refuse to purify yourself, and remain with suffering.

Give up all self-seeking; give up self, and the Peace of God will be yours!

No Fear In Love

The supreme law of life is love, an unconditional and everlasting love.

If you become one with that love, by loving all with your mind free from all hatred, you shall receive an invincible protection which only love can give. This kind of unconditional love will amaze you.

The children of light, who abide in the Kingdom of Heaven, see the universe and all that it contains as the manifestation of one law, the law of love. They see love as sustaining, protecting, and a perfecting power eminent in all things animate and inanimate.

To them, love is not merely a rule; it is the law of life itself. Knowing this, they order their whole life in accordance with love.

By practicing obedience to the highest, to divine love, we may become conscious partakers of the power of love, and so arrive at perfect freedom. The universe is preserved because love is at the heart of it. Love is the only true preservative power we have.

While there is hatred in the hearts of people, they imagine the law to be cruel, but when their hearts are mellowed by compassion and love, they perceive that the law is an infinite kindness.

Arriving at love, one enters into full possession of body and mind, by right of God's divine power manifested within us.

"Perfect love casts out fear."

To know the law of love is to know that there is no harmful power in the whole universe. Nothing can harm your spirit.

Even sin itself, which the worldly and unbelieving imagine is so unconquerable, is known as a very weak and perishable thing, that shrinks away and disappears before the compelling power of good.

Perfect love is perfect patience. Anger and irritability cannot dwell with it or come near it. Love can sweeten every bitter occasion with the perfume of holiness and transforms trials into divine strength.

When we truly love unconditionally, we tend to suffer no more, because we accept all things and conditions and we are constantly blessed. Loss and sorrow does not overtake us because we understand that perfect love is perfect trust. When we have removed the desire to grasp at possessions, we can never be troubled with the fear of loss.

When we maintain a loving attitude of mind toward all people and things in the constant performance of our duties and loving activity, we will find that love protects and supplies all our needs.

Perfect love is perfect power and perfect wisdom. The person, who loves having thoroughly learned the lessons of their own heart, knows and understands the tasks and trials of other hearts.

Love succeeds where the intellect fails; sees where the intellect is blind; knows where the intellect is ignorant. Reason is only completed in love, and is ultimately absorbed in it.

Infinite tenderness enfolds and cherishes the universe; we become gentle, childlike and tender- hearted. Understanding that the one thing, which all creatures need, is love.

To the eye of love, all things are revealed in the light of eternal principles, out of which spring all causes and effects, and back into which they return.

"God is Love;" there is nothing more perfect. He who would find pure knowledge let him find pure love.

Perfect love is perfect peace. Immerse your whole being in the light of love each day.

He who dwells with it has completed their journey in the underworld of sorrow.

Christ taught love, kindness, and charity. One of the beautiful things in the Bible is the parable of the Good Samaritan told by Jesus in Luke 10:25–37.

On one occasion an expert in the law stood up to test Jesus. "Teacher," he asked, "What must I do to inherit eternal life?" Jesus said to him, "What is written in the Law? What do you read there?" The man answered, "'Love the Lord your God. Love him with all your heart, all your soul, all your strength, and all your mind." Also, "You must 'Love your neighbor as you love yourself." Jesus said to him, "Your answer is right. Do this and you will have life forever."

But the man wanted to show that the way he was living was right. So he said to Jesus, "And who is my neighbor?" In reply, Jesus said: "A man was going down the road from Jerusalem to Jericho when he was attacked by robbers. They tore off his clothes and beat him. Then they left him lying there almost dead. A priest happened to be going down the same road, and when he saw the man, he passed by on the other side of the road. Next, a Levite came there; he went over and looked at the man. Then he walked by on the other side of the road.

But a Samaritan, as he traveled, came where the hurt man was lying. He saw the man and felt very sorry for him. He went to him and bandaged his wounds, pouring on oil and wine. Then he put the man on his own donkey, brought him to an inn and took care of him.

The next day he took out two silver coins and gave them to the innkeeper. The Samaritan said, "Take care of this man. If you spend more money on him, I will pay it back to you when I come again"

Then Jesus said, "Which of these three men do you think was a neighbor to the

man who was attacked by the robbers?"
The expert in the law replied, "The one
who helped him." Jesus told him, "Then go
and do the same thing he did."

Here is one of my favorite Bible verses I
actually memorized once, I wrote it down
every day for three weeks. I have to do it
again soon.

Love is patient, love is kind, it does not
envy, it does not boast, it is not proud. It
does not dishonor others, it is not self-
seeking, it is not easily angered, it keeps
no record of wrongs. Love does not delight
in evil but rejoices with the truth. It
always protects, always trusts, always
hopes, always perseveres. Love never fails.
- *1 Corinthians 13*

Serenity

The calmness of mind is one of the most beautiful jewels of wisdom. Beautiful thinking is the result of long and patient effort in self-control. Its presence is an indication of ripened experience and more than ordinary knowledge of the laws and operations of thought.

You become calm in the measure that you understand yourself as a thought evolved being, for such knowledge necessitates the understanding of others and as you develop a right understanding, you will see more clearly, all the internal relations of things by the action of cause and effect.

You will then cease to worry or grieve; you will remain poised, steadfast and become cheerful. Overlooking the small things. Having learned how to govern yourself, you will know how to adapt yourself to others; and they, in turn, will respect your spiritual strength and feel that they can rely on you.

The more tranquil you become, the greater your success. Even your co-workers will watch your business prosperity increase and promotions come your way as you develop a greater self-control and calmness. People will always prefer to deal with someone whose demeanor is good-natured and kind.

The strong, calm person is always loved and revered. You are like a shade-giving tree in a thirsty land or a sheltering rock in a storm. "Who does not love a tranquil heart with a sweet-tempered, balanced life?

It does not matter whether it rains or shines, or what changes come to those possessing these blessings, for they are always sweet, serene, and calm.

That exquisite poise of character, which we call serenity, is the last lesson of culture, the abundance of the soul. It is as precious as wisdom, more to be desired than gold. How insignificant mere money seeking looks in comparison with a serene life, a life that dwells in the ocean of truth, beneath the waves, beyond the reach of tempests, in the eternal calm!

How many people do you know who have ruined their lives and all that is beautiful by explosive tempers, some have even destroyed their character, and made bad blood between themselves and others?

Yes, humanity surges with uncontrolled anger and division, and at times we are disrupted with uncontrollable grief. All of which is understandable with us who have lost loved ones or have been suddenly struck with tragedy.

There are those who blame others and live with grudges; some will find themselves with incurable ailments. I would like to add that if certain diseases or ailments are in our DNA from former generations, all we can do is live out our days the best we can. With the ability and knowledge to control our thoughts and feelings with patience. Only those whose thoughts are controlled and purified makes the winds and the storms of the soul obey.

Calmness is power. Forgiving others is the key to better health and a sound mind. We all know certain people that are difficult to be around. It feels like work, it takes patience to deal with them.

Aristotle had an interesting thing to say I thought to include, "It is the mark of an educated mind to be able to entertain a thought without accepting it."

How few people we meet in life who are well balanced, who have that exquisite poise which is characteristic of the finished character!

Worrying, fretting, every dishonest act, every feeling of envy, jealousy and fear has its own effect on your system, and in effect becomes contaminated like a poison or a deformer of the body.

Mental Scientists emphasize personal development as the vehicle to awaken ones' latent abilities. "Every small stroke of virtue or vice leaves its, ever so little scar. Nothing we ever do is wiped out.

Say to your own heart, "Peace, be still!" Every emotion tends to sculpt the body into beauty or into ugliness. This is true of all of our attributes. A person's face is marred with wrinkles and lines that mark their true disposition through life and as they get older, these demarcations set in and show the true character of their heart.

The way to be beautiful is to be beautiful within by Beautiful Thinking. One who is filled with joy and gratefulness will have a future of blessedness and serenity.

Aspiration

On the wings of aspiration, we rise from earth to heaven, from ignorance to knowledge, from darkness to light.

The lover of the pure life renews their mind daily with the invigorating glow of aspiration. Rising early helps to fortify your mind with strong thoughts and strenuous endeavor.

Did you know that the mind is of such a nature that it cannot remain for a moment unoccupied and that if it is not held and guided by high thoughts and pure aspirations, it will assuredly be enslaved and misguided by low thoughts and base desires?

Our aspirations can be nurtured and encouraged by our daily habits. Aspiration can be sought and admitted into your mind as a divine guide, or it can be neglected and shut out. To retire for a short time each day to some quiet spot, preferably in the open air, and call up the energies of the mind in surging waves of holy rapture, is to prepare the mind for great spiritual victories and destinies of divine import. For such rapture is the preparation for wisdom and the prelude to peace.

Before your mind can contemplate pure things it must be lifted up to them, it must rise above impure things; and aspiration is the instrument by which this is all accomplished. By its aid, your mind soars swiftly and surely into heavenly places and begins to experience divine things. It begins to accumulate wisdom and learns to guide itself by an increasing measure of the divine light of pure knowledge.

To thirst for righteousness; to hunger for the pure life; to rise in holy rapture on the wings of angelic aspiration, this is the right path to wisdom. This is the right striving for peace. This is the right beginning of the way divine.

106

Evil and good cannot dwell together. Evil must be abandoned, left behind and transcended before the good is grasped and known. When good is practiced and fully comprehended, then all the afflictions of the mind are at an end.

The strong traveler on the highway of truth knows no such thing as resignation to evil; he knows only obedience to good.

The lover of good is not a lover of evil, neither can he, for one moment, admit its control. He elevates and glorifies good, not evil. He loves the light, not the darkness.

All in all, when divine good is practiced, life is bliss. Bliss is the normal condition of the good man or woman. Completely aware of others lack of power over you. You are free.

And what are the transcendent virtues that embody all happiness and joy within? They are for one, impartiality; the seeing so deeply into the human heart, and into human actions, that it becomes almost impossible to take sides with someone or one party against the other, and therefore the self-control to be perfectly just.

What we need is unlimited kindness towards all men, women, and all creatures, whether enemies or friends.

Try to develop and perfect patience at all times, in all circumstances, and under the severest trials. It takes practice. Patience is not something you can just get more of, it is something you have to put on. Let me explain further.

Leonardo da Vinci wrote a wonderful quote to share with others, he said, "Patience serves as a protection against wrongs as clothes do against cold. For if you put on more clothes as the cold increases, it will have no power to hurt you."

Take for example, when it is really cold outside, you will put on your coat, hat, gloves, a scarf and perhaps warm boots.

So in like manner, you must grow in patience when you meet with great wrongs or when people are testing your patience.

You will mentally put on these clothes of patience visually in your mind, as they are talking too loud, or projecting, blaming, or angry, they will be powerless to vex your mind and upset you.

You don't have to be a victim of other people's negative insults or projections. You can build an invisible shield around yourself. You can be more than a survivor; you can become victorious in your life.

Have perfect peace toward all. Be at peace with the world. Every soul is in need of peace, and it varies with different individuals, but there is not one soul that does not feel it to some degree.

Every soul, consciously or unconsciously, hungers for righteousness, and every soul seeks to gratify that hunger in its own particular way, and in accordance with its own particular state of knowledge.

Having compassion for all creatures and people in their sufferings. Abounding love toward all living things; rejoicing with the happy and successful, and sympathizing with the sorrowful and defeated.

Such are the virtues that transcend both vice and attributes. They include all that virtue embodies while going beyond it into divine truth. They are the fruits of our efforts to achieve the glorious gifts of one who overcomes.

Those who seek divine truth consciously will be blessed, they shall find that final and permanent satisfaction of the soul which only true righteousness can give, for they will come into the knowledge of the true path.

The great need of the soul is called righteousness, on which it may stand securely where it may build the mansion of a beautiful, peaceful, and perfect life.

It is the realization of this principle where the Kingdom of Heaven, the abiding home of the soul resides, and the source of every permanent blessing.

In finding it, all is found; not finding it, all is lost. It is an attitude of mind, a state of consciousness in which the struggle for existence ceases, and the soul finds itself at rest in the midst of plenty, where its great need is satisfied without worry and without fear. Imagine living in a world of inner peace.

It is best to be superior to all your worldly possessions and the opinions of others. Once you have overcome the opinions of others you will be wise.

One who identifies themselves with their possessions will feel that all is lost when their possessions are lost. Having this wisdom, you will be the same whether in riches or poverty. The one will not add to your strength or rob you of your serenity.

Imagine detaching yourself from every outward thing, and to rest securely upon your inward virtue, this is unfailing wisdom.

It's important to know who you are. It is your character that determines who you are. You alone choose what your character shall be. How do you know what your character is? Are you a person who is kind, considerate, loyal and loving, or are you jealous and self-absorbed?.

Identifying yourself by what you do for your career could be a mistake. What if a setback, accident or ailment were to prevent you from doing what you do, then who are you? You can refuse to be enslaved by any outward thing or happening, by regarding all such things and happenings, for your use and for your education. This is a form of wisdom.

To the wise person, all occurrences are good, and, having no eye for evil, they grow wiser every day. They utilize all things and therefore put all things under their feet. They see all their mistakes as soon as made, and accept them as lessons of intrinsic value and move on.

They are moved by none, yet learn from all. They crave love from none yet give love to all. To learn, and not to be shaken, to love where one is not loved: herein lies the strength, which shall never fail a man or woman.

To love the unlovable and accept them as they are is sometimes difficult; it may be a family member or friend that has never gotten over their childhood trauma or past trials. They may live their childhood traumas in the present, going over it again and again or they may be dealing with dementia where there is no filter for what might be said out loud by them. This is where understanding and patience play their part in your mind and heart.

As you care for them, you may experience your own feelings becoming hurt and upset, you may want to help them to change their attitude but it may be a challenge. Perhaps by reading this book to them by candlelight may help. Letting the light shine in the darkness always helps every situation.

All strength, wisdom, power and divine knowledge we have to understand and find within ourselves.

We will not find wisdom in egotism; we will only find it in obedience, submission and the willingness to learn. We must obey the higher, and not glorify ourselves in the lower. If we stand upon egotism, rejecting instruction and the lessons of experience, we will surely fall.

We can be supportive for one another, but we cannot be strong for them. We can pray for them but we can only be strong for ourselves; we cannot overcome for another, we can only overcome obstacles and emotions for ourselves.

Put away all external props, and rely upon the truth within you. A speculative philosophy will prove a shadowy thing in the time of calamity; a person must have inner wisdom, which puts an end to grief. When we accept our sorrow in can turn to peace.

There is immense power in acceptance; we will never overcome the things that we deny. Take some time to take a mental inventory of what you feel and think about things. What holds you back and what or who is affecting your deepest feelings.

Accept what you cannot change and change the things you can. Let the peace that surpasses understanding fill your heart and mind.

Unfailing wisdom is found only by constant practice in pure thinking and by harmonizing your mind and heart to those things that are beautiful, lovable, and true. The yearning after rewards and the fear of punishment should be put away forever.

Let a person joyfully lean towards the faithful performance of all their duties, forgetting worthless pleasures, living self-contained and then they will surely find wisdom.

When circumstances, or persons, arouse either resentment or resistance in us, let us ignore the circumstances or persons until we have quieted ourselves with more compassion and patience. Some people just know how to push out hot buttons. Sometimes, it's more than we want to deal with and we try to avoid them. We can only take them in small doses.

When you are confronted with negative emotional feelings and it causes you to react with a less than wonderful attitude, think of the attitude as a bad outfit, take it off, throw it on the floor and kick it out of the way. Been there, done that... no more!

Form a habit of having great expectations; it will awaken the potential for them to become your reality. It's a great thing to realize that freedom from the bondage of difficult issues and circumstances is not only possible but that loving, intellectual freedom will lead us from goodness to greatness, giving us more vitality to every action of our lives.

"In almost everything that touches our everyday life on earth, God is pleased when we're pleased. He wills that we be as free as birds to soar and sing our maker's praise without anxiety."
- *A. W. Tozer*

Body and Mind

Just as an artist becomes by practice accomplished in their craft, so you can become, by practice, accomplished in Beautiful Thinking. It is entirely a matter of forming new habits of thought.

It will be seen that the first step in the discipline of the mind is the overcoming of procrastination or laziness.

This is the easiest step, and until it is perfectly accomplished, the other steps cannot be taken. Laziness consists in giving the body more ease and sleep than it requires, in procrastinating we find we are neglecting those things, which should receive immediate attention.

This condition must be overcome by rousing up the body at an early hour, giving it just the amount of sleep it requires for complete regeneration, and by doing promptly every task or duty, no matter how small, as it comes along.

The next step is the overcoming of self-indulgence or gluttony. The glutton is he who eats for self-gratification only, without considering the effects. He eats more than his body requires, and is greedy of sweet things and rich dishes.

These undisciplined desires can only be overcome by reducing the quantity of food we eat, and the number of meals per day.

Regular hours should be set apart for meals, and eating at other times should be avoided. I know it's hard to do at times in this busy world we live in, but you can try.

It has been proven that a smaller meal before seven in the evening is best or even at times when dinner is skipped if you really want to lose weight. At one time, large dinners were considered altogether unnecessary, promoting heavy sleep and cloudiness of mind. Like eating a big dish of pasta with sourdough bread and butter. I'm Italian, so this is a tough one for me.

Anyway, the pursuit of such a method of discipline will rapidly bring your appetite under control, and as the sensual sin of self-indulgence is taken out of the mind, the right selection of foods will be instinctively and infallibly adapted to the purified mental condition.

It should be well established in mind that a change of heart is the needful thing, and that any change in your diet that does not promote this end will not work.

When the body is exercised and firmly guided, early rising becomes a delight and abstinence firmly established in the heart. Then the foundation of a poised, virtuous life is possible.

Self-control comes in different forms, some impulsive, some physical, some emotional.

Having self-control in body and mind when it pertains to others is most important, especially when it comes to giving advice. Something to remember is to wait for someone to ask you for your advice. Think of it in these terms, when someone wants to know what time it is, they will ask you for it. Can you imagine someone going around telling everybody what time it is like the town crier? It would probably not happen very often today as most everyone has the time at his or her fingertips. You get the point.

Self-control involves holding your tongue when you know you should not share personal information about someone. When you yourself are in a predicament that involves other people and looking for advice, it is not considered gossip or slander.

Slander consists of inventing or repeating unkind and evil reports about others, in exposing and magnifying the faults of others, or absent friends, and in spreading unworthy insinuations.

Remember, if you are part of the story, then it is not gossip.

Slander always intends to hurt and destroy others. The elements of insincerity, shame and untruthfulness enter into every slanderous act. One who aims at living a righteous life will begin to check any cruel words of slander before they have gone out from their mouth and then eliminate the insincere thought. Take your thoughts captive. It is better to say nothing.

We have to watch out for and refrain from defaming, and condemning the absent friend, whose face we have so recently smiled into or kissed, or whose hand we have shaken. We must not say of another that which we dare not say to their face. Idle speech consists in talking about the private affairs of others, in talking merely to pass away the time, and in engaging in aimless and irrelevant conversation

The person of virtue and wisdom will hold their tongue and not let it run on foolishly, but will make their speech strong and pure with a purpose or remain silent.

Most times silence is best. When one is inclined to curse, and condemn others, let them restrain themselves and look within.

The virtuous person refrains from all abusive language and quarreling. They speak only words that are useful, necessary, pure, and true. It has been said that people who swear a lot have a smaller vocabulary and are not able to speak intelligently about a situation. Unless some driver pulls out in front of you and almost causes an accident. It's hard not to react, well...as long as they don't hear you.

Life is short and whoever is on the watch to catch the words of others, in order to contradict them, has yet to reach the higher way of Beautiful Thinking.

The person who is always on the alert to check their own words in order to soften and purify them will find the higher way and the truer life.

Natural Sleep

Sleeping, like breathing and digesting, is controlled by the subconscious brain centers. Natural sleep requires no positive mental impulse; it's just relaxing, and nature takes care of the process.

That is natural sleep, but when you start your dry cell battery, the brain, and begin to worry and get angry that you are going to stay awake and never get to sleep. Then the conscious mind begins to dominate the subconscious mind, and you destroy the very comfort you seek to have.

The fear of insomnia, the over-anxiety to go to sleep, is to be more dreaded than insomnia itself. To get the refreshing sleep you must put yourself in a state of actual physical tiredness.

Get some exercise. Walk in one direction until the first symptoms of becoming tired appear, then walk home. Take a hot bath or shower. Open your windows to let in some fresh air, then relax. Don't worry; you are going to get some sleep.

Lie on your back, open your eyes wide, look up as if you were trying to see your eyebrows, hold your eyes open this way ten to twenty seconds, then close them slowly. Repeat this several times. It will definitely make you tired.

Sleep will have descended on you before you realize it. Occupy your mind with autosuggestions like this: "I am going to sleep sound tonight, I will have restful, peaceful sleep. My eyelids are getting heavy, very heavy. I am going to close them and go to sleep." Relax all the parts of your body.

If these suggestions do not help you the first night, say: "All right, my brain was too active; tomorrow I will try again and relax my body more, starting at my toes to my head." Next night eat one or two dry crackers; chew them slowly and this little bit of food will draw the blood pressure from the brain and help you to go to sleep.

Drive out business and worry thoughts. Think faith and courage thoughts.

When you pray, pray the perfect prayer, "The Our Father" when you do, and when you say the words, think of those you love and forgive... see their faces in your mind. As you pray the words, forgive us our trespasses, etc. You will be praying for their provision and lives as well. Pray it and think about it. It is awesome.

Like most of us we end the evening with Netflix or some type of movie. Make a change one evening and try to finish your evening with a chapter in a book that is interesting, yet educational. Let the last pages you read at night be something worth storing up in that precious brain of yours, and the good, worth-while deposit will grow and produce beautiful worth-while mental fruit.

Goodness and Greatness

All greatness springs from goodness and goodness is profoundly simple, without goodness there is no greatness.

Some people pass through the world as destructive forces, like a tornado or an avalanche. They cause us deep emotional scars, making us think we are the cause and reason they act that way toward us.

You may have a relative or someone who tries to insult or abuse you and afterwards they say, "Now, look at what you made me do!" Have you ever experienced someone saying that to you? I am here to tell you, "Don't own it." Don't believe it for a second! These people are to greatness as the avalanche is to the mountain.

The work of greatness is enduring and preservative and not violent or destructive. The greatest souls are the most gentle. Greatness is acquired by being humble; a good way to practice humility is to spend more time listening than you do talking. Don't try to compare yourself with other people, instead, show your appreciation for the talents and qualities of others. Put others before you and remain teachable, seek guidance in books and from mentors.

Greatness is never obtrusive. It works in silence, seeking no recognition. Greatness is humble. This is why it is not easily perceived and recognized. Only after spending time with a person who has this type of greatness will you have an idea of this kind of wisdom and power.

Like the mountain, it towers up in its vastness, so that those in its immediate vicinity, who receive its shelter and shade, do not see it. Its sublime grandeur is admired as they move back away from it.

People mostly occupy themselves with things like their jobs, houses, politics and new technology, and a few contemplate the mountain at whose base they live.

But in the distance, these small things disappear, and then the solitary beauty of the mountain is perceived. Popularity and shallowness, these superficialities rapidly disappear leaving behind no enduring mark. True greatness slowly emerges from stardom and endures forever.

All true genius is impersonal. It belongs not to the man and woman through whom it is manifested; it belongs to all. It is a diffusion of pure truth, the light of heaven descending on all.

Every work of genius, in whatever department of art, is a symbolic manifestation of impersonal truth. It is universal and finds a response in every heart in every age and race. Anything short of this is not genius or greatness.

The greatest art is, like nature, artless. It knows no trick, no pose or studied effort. There are no stage-tricks in Shakespeare, and he is the greatest of dramatists because he is the simplest.

The so-called critics, who do not fully understand the wise simplicity of this type of greatness, always condemn the most brilliant work. They cannot discriminate between the childish and the childlike.

The true, the beautiful, the great, is always childlike and is perennially fresh and young. The great man is always simple. He draws from and lives in the inexhaustible fountain of divine goodness within.

"It is as easy to be great as to be small," says Emerson; and he utters a profound truth. Forgetfulness of self is the whole of greatness, as it is the whole of goodness and happiness. In a fleeting moment of self-forgetfulness the smallest soul becomes great; extend that moment indefinitely, and there is a great soul, a great life.

Heaven In The Heart

When your mind is harmonized with the divine law of love, the wheel of drudgery ceases to turn and all work is transmuted into joyful activity. The labor of life ceases when the heart is pure.

The pure-hearted are like the lilies of the field, which toil not, yet are fed and clothed from the abundant storehouse of heaven. So is it with those who, having yielded up self-will, grow in humility, grace, goodness, and beauty, freed from anxiety.

Heaven is everywhere. It is wherever there is a pure heart. The whole universe is abounding with joy, but the sin-bound heart cannot see, hear or partake of it.

The golden gates of heaven are eternally open, but the selfish cannot find them; they mourn, yet see not; they cry, but hear not. Only to those who turn their eyes upward toward heavenly things and their ears to heavenly sounds, are the happy portals of the kingdom revealed, and they enter and are glad. Take time to meditate on this. Keep your eyes towards the hills and think higher thoughts.

I stayed at the Fairmont Hotel in San Jose, CA for my 40th birthday. In the morning as I woke up, I could hear music as if it were right outside my window, but my room was on the fourteenth floor of the hotel. To my surprise as I looked outside, I saw a band performing at the park below. This confirmed to me that all sound actually rises and everything we say must rise up and be heard in heaven. So now, I am even more careful of what words I speak. I just have to be better at it when driving.

All life is gladness when the heart is right when it is attuned to the sweet chords of holy love. Love sees with faultless vision and acts in wisdom. Look through the eyes of love, and you shall see everywhere the beautiful that judge with the mind of love.

To love all and always, this is the heaven of heavens. "Let there be nothing within you that is not beautiful and gentle, and then will there be nothing that is not beautified and softened by the spell of your presence." All that you do, let it be done in calm wisdom, and not from desire, impulse, or opinion; this is the heavenly way of action.

Purify your thought-world until no stain is left, and you will ascend into heaven while living in the body. You will then see the things of the outward world clothed in all beautiful forms.

Undeveloped souls are merely unopened flowers. The perfect beauty lies concealed within, and will one day reveal itself to the fully orbed light of heaven.

He who loves becomes the protector of all. What gardener is so foolish as to condemn his flowers because they do not develop in a day?

Come and live in the sunshine of your being. Come out of the shadows and the dark places. You are a child of heaven. Be a child of purity, wisdom, love, joy, and peace, these are the eternal realities of the kingdom within, and they are yours, but you cannot possess them in sin; they have no part in the realm of darkness.

Your mind is the infallible weaver of your destiny. Your mind clothes itself in garments of its own making. We learn by experience.

It is the nature of the mind to create its own conditions, and we ourselves choose the state of consciousness in which our mind shall dwell. Our minds also have the power to alter any condition, to abandon any state. This it is continually doing as it gathers knowledge of attitude after attitude by repeated choice and exhaustive experience. Temptation does not arise in the outer object, but in the lust of the mind for that object. Neither does sorrow and suffering belong by nature to the external things and happenings of life but in an undisciplined attitude of mind toward those things and happenings. The way of enlightenment and peace is not gained by assuming authority and guidance over other minds, but by exercising a lawful authority over one's own mind, and by guiding one's self in pathways of steadfast and lofty virtue.

A woman's life proceeds from her heart and mind. She has compounded that mind by her own thoughts and deeds. It is within her power to refashion her mind by her choice of thought. In this manner, she can transform her life.

Truth be told, when it comes to meeting someone you are attracted to, don't try to be what you think they might want in a person, don't pretend, be who you really are. Just be you or you will end up deceiving yourself. Pretending to be someone or something more than you are is the foolish path to take; it will only frustrate you and end the relationship in misery.

Be the best you can be. Here is an analogy I learned quite early in life that helped me to gain more self-esteem. Let's say you were like a plum, you could be perfect in shape, color and size, and really sweet. Well, not everybody likes plums, some people like bananas, so you could try to be a banana, so those people will like you, but you would only be a second rate banana. So, why not be the best plum you could possibly be.

Falling into a relationship on false pretenses is like being a second rate banana and lying about your true character is not good, for the character is simply defined by what you will do or won't do. Where do you draw the line?

All of us have the power to form harmful habits. Remember, both equally have the same power to create habits that are essentially good. It is commonly said by those with a lack of conscience, that it is easier to do wrong than right. That it is easier to sin rather than to be holy, such a condition has come to be regarded, almost universally, as a self-evident truth. That is why our prisons are full, the outcome of bad choices.

It is the same in the vital things of mind and life. To think and do right requires much practice and renewed effort.

But the time comes at last when it becomes habitual and easy to think and do right, and difficult to do that which is wrong.

A simple thing like, when a child is learning to write, it is extremely easy to hold the pen wrong and to form letters incorrectly, but it is painfully difficult to hold the pen and to write properly. This is because of the child's ignorance of the art of writing, which can only be resolved by effort and practice until it becomes easy to hold the pen correctly. The person teaching them should hold the pen with them in their hand and help them to write correctly.

Everything takes time and practice, the sooner you begin whatever it is you want to learn, become or change about yourself, the easier it gets.

Higher Life

Having prepared our heart and mind by overcoming the more surface and chaotic conditions mentioned in previous chapters we now come to some important things to know and remember.

Here are some of the leading wrong mental conditions and their disastrous effects upon one's life.

These are negative conditions to be replaced by positive and loving thoughts.

Hatred - which leads to injury, violence, disaster, and suffering.

Lust - which leads to confusion of intellect, remorse, shame, and wretchedness.

Covetousness - which leads to fear, unrest, unhappiness, and loss.

Pride - which leads to disappointment, humiliation, and lack of self-knowledge.

Vanity - which leads to distress and mortification of spirit.

Condemnation - which leads to persecution and hatred from others.

Self-indulgence - which leads to misery, loss of judgment, grossness, disease, and neglect.

Anger - which leads to the loss of power and influence.

The above wrong conditions of mind are states of darkness and deprivation and not of positive power. The hater is one who has failed to understand the lesson of love correctly and suffers in consequence.

When one succeeds in doing right, the hatred will have disappeared. We cannot remain empty from within; we have to replace the bad thoughts with the good.

The following are the more important right mental conditions and their beneficial effects upon your life:

Love - which leads to gentle conditions, bliss, and blessedness.

Purity - which leads to intellectual clearness, joy and invincible confidence.

Selflessness - which leads to courage, satisfaction, happiness, and abundance.

Humility - which leads to calmness, restfulness, and knowledge of truth.

Gentleness - which leads to emotional equilibrium and contentment under all circumstances.

Compassion - which leads to protection, love, and reverence from others.

Goodwill - which leads to gladness and success.

Self-control - which leads to peace of mind, true judgment, refinement, health, and honor.

Patience - which leads to mental power and far reaching influence.

The above right conditions of mind are states of positive power, light, joyful possession, and knowledge.

They will aspire to the attainment of the higher life in its completion and perceive with unveiled vision the true order of things and the meaning of life.

It's time to abandon all the wrong conditions of the heart, and persevere unceasingly in the practice of good.

Start by doing what's necessary; then do what's possible; and suddenly you are doing the impossible
- *Francis of Assisi*

Victorious and Confident

To be a conqueror in appearance is the first step toward success. It inspires confidence in others as well as in oneself.

Walk, talk and act as though you were someone people would want to know, and you are more likely to become such.

Move about among your friends as though you believe you are already a person of importance. Let victory speak from your face and express itself in your manner.

Carry yourself like someone who is conscious of what's going on around and has an impressive mission, a grand aim in life. Radiate a hopeful, expectant, cheerful atmosphere.

In other words, be a good advertisement of the winner you are going to be. I'm not saying to walk around like a rooster making a lot of noise. Being and acting as though you are already successful in life without telling it to everyone you meet is the key. Be confident, yet humble. Just be. You have a purpose in your heart.

A victorious expression inspires trust and makes a favorable impression upon others. Remember, a despondent, discouraged expression creates distrust and makes an unfavorable impression.

It is difficult to get very far away from people's assessment of us. A bad first impression often creates a prejudice that may be impossible to remove.

The world has little use for whiners or long-faced failures. People will turn a deaf ear to your plea for work. No matter if you are jobless and have been out of work for a long time you must keep up a winning appearance, a victorious attitude, or you will lose the very thing you are after.

Not that we should deceive by trying to appear what we are not, but we should always keep our best side out, not our second best or our worst.

Besides, when you go for a job interview, you are interviewing the employer as much as they are interviewing you. If you think about it, they are not just looking at your experience or talents; they want to get to know you and see if your attitude and personality would fit in with theirs and the others you would work with. If the person interviewing you is not someone you would want to see five days a week or even know, look for another job.

Our personal appearance is our show window that displays who and what we are, and we are judged by what we put there.

The importance of radiating a cheerful attitude with a smile will be honored and remembered. A smile is internationally understood everywhere we go.

The victorious idea of life is the thing to keep uppermost in the mind, for it is this that will lead you to the light. You must give the impression that you are a success, or that you have qualities that will make you successful, that you are making good, or no recommendation or testimonial however strong will counteract the unfavorable impression you might otherwise make.

So much of our progress in life depends upon our reputation, upon making a favorable impression upon others, that it is of the utmost importance to cultivate mental forcefulness.

It is the mind that colors the personality and gives it its tone and character. If we cultivate willpower, decision and positive thinking instead of negative thinking, we cannot help but make an impression of masterfulness, and everybody knows that this is the qualification that accomplishes things.

It is masterfulness that achieves results, and if we do not express it in our appearance, people will not have confidence in our achieving ability. They may think that we can sell goods behind a counter, work under orders, carry out some mechanical routine with faithfulness and precision, but they will not think we are fit for leadership or that we can command resources to meet possible crises or big emergencies.

Never say or do anything which will show the earmarks of a weakling, or of a failure. Never permit yourself to assume a poverty-stricken attitude. Never admit by your speech, your appearance, your gait, your manner, that there is anything wrong with you.

The majority of people seem to take it for granted that life is a great gambling game in which the odds are rigged against them. This conviction colors their whole attitude and is responsible for failure.

Hold up your head. Walk erect. Walk as thought you had a balloon tied to each shoulder lifting you up straight.

Look everybody in the face. No matter how poor you may be, or how shabby your clothes, whether you are jobless, homeless, or friendless. Show the world that you respect yourself, and that you believe in yourself. No matter how hard life is for you, keep marching on to victory. Show by your expression that you can think and plan for yourself, that you have a forceful mentality. The victorious, triumphant attitude will put you in command of resources you need, whereas a timid, self-depreciating, failure attitude will drive those very things away from you.

Our mental outlook determines our manner and our appearance. If we see only failure ahead, we will act and look like failures. We have already failed.

If we expect success, if we see it waiting for us a little bit up the road, we will act and look like successes. We have already succeeded. The failure attitude loses; the victorious attitude wins. Thinking of yourself as habitually lucky will tend to make you so, just as thinking of yourself as habitually unlucky and always talking about your failures and your cruel fate will tend to make you unlucky.

Laughter

The power of laughter is a gift given to serve a wise purpose in our lives. It is nature's device for exercising the internal organs and giving us pleasure at the same time.

Laughter begins in the lungs and diaphragm, setting the internal organs into a quick, jelly-like vibration, which gives a pleasant sensation almost equal to that of horseback riding.

During digestion, the movements of the stomach are similar to churning. Every time you take a full breath, or when you laugh out loud, the diaphragm descends and gives the stomach an extra squeeze and shakes it.

Frequent laughing sets the stomach to dancing, speeding up the digestive process. The heart beats faster, and sends the blood bounding through the body. Laughter accelerates the respiration, and gives warmth and glow to the whole system. It brightens the eyes and tends to restore that exquisite poise or balance which we call healthy, harmonious actions of all the functions of the body.

This delicate composure may be destroyed by a sleepless night, a piece of bad news or by mere anxiety and often restored by a good hearty laugh or two. Here are a few anonymous jokes for a laugh, etc.

A child asked his father, "How were people born?" So his father said, "Adam and Eve made babies, then their babies became adults and made babies, and so on." The child then went to his mother, asked her the same question and she told him, "We were monkeys then we evolved to become like we are now." The child ran back to his father and said, "You lied to me!" His father replied, "No, your mom was talking about her side of the family."

Here's one more for the kids...

Teacher: "If I gave you two cats and another two cats and another two, how many would you have?"

Johnny: "Seven."

Teacher: "No, listen carefully... If I gave you two cats, and another two cats and another two, how many would you have?"

Johnny: "Seven."

Teacher: "Let me put it to you differently. If I gave you two apples, and another two apples and another two, how many would you have?"

Johnny: "Six."

Teacher: "Good. Now if I gave you two cats, and another two cats and another two, how many would you have?"

Johnny: "Seven!"

Teacher: "Johnny, where in the heck do you get seven from?"

Johnny: "Because I've already got a freaking cat!"

Making Others Happy

Do something for someone; making others happy is a positive way to live and a guarantee of your own happiness.

We have all had obstacles and rough times in our lives. Someone who we could learn a lesson from would be Paul in the Bible. He had trials, setbacks, hardships and hard labors; he had defeats and discouragements and still, the record shows he was "always rejoicing."

Paul was a prisoner in a dungeon, he sang songs and rejoiced. He kept a light in his heart and he was always happy, not because he struggled to find happiness, but because he had dedicated his life to the service of others.

The real hero, the person of fame and popularity, doesn't arrive by setting out on a quest for any of these things; the result is incidental. The real hero forgets self first of all; an essential step to greatness.

Lincoln, the tired nobleman in his speech at Gettysburg, never dreamed that that speech would stamp him as a master of words and thought in the hearts of his countrymen.

He thought not of himself. He was trying to soothe wounds, cheer troubled spirits, and give courage to those who had been so long in desolation.

I am often asked: "Are you happy ALL the time?" My answer is no.

Any human being cannot enjoy a continuous state of happiness. There are no plans, no habits or methods of living that will ensure unbroken happiness.

Happiness means periods or marking posts in our journey along life's road. These high points of bliss are enjoyed because we have to walk through the low places at times. There will be times people anger you and you have a choice to respond or not. Most times it is best to turn the other cheek.

We need the night to make us enjoy the day, winter to make us enjoy summer, clouds to make us enjoy the sunshine, sorrow to make us enjoy happiness.

Being content is the magic lamp in life, according to the beautiful picture painted for us by Goethe, transforming the rude fisherman's hut into a palace of silver; the logs, the floors, the roof, the furniture, everything is changed and gleaming with new light.

When you have the blues or sorrow, or when you have worry or trouble, it's the time to get a hold on your thinking machinery and erase the shadows that cross your path.

At times when I have memories or visions of hurtful times, I imagine they are on a blackboard in pictures and I grab an eraser and mentally erase them.

Focus your thoughts on your blessings;
these are the wonderful methods to apply.
As I have stated before, gratefulness is the
key.

As long as you dwell upon your imagined
or your real sorrows, you will find yourself
miserable, the anxiety and worries will
magnify like a thunderstorm.

Change your thoughts to confidence, faith,
and good cheer.

"Faith, in the sense in which I am here
using the word, is the art of holding on to
things your reason has once accepted, in
spite of your changing moods."
- *C.S. Lewis*

Think of the happiest times you have ever
had. When trouble or sorrows come,
sweeten your mind with remembrances of
joys that have been and joys coming to
you. Envy no one; envy breeds worry.
The person you would envy has their
sorrows and shadows, too. You see them

only when the sunlight is on their face; you don't see them when they are down or stressed for the most part.

Some people who have more than they need, have to rent storage for things they haven't seen in years. They have more bills and worries over things being stolen. They have to pay for insurance on everything. There is no need to envy anyone.

Living in faith and gratefulness will give you a heart full of love and joy, no matter what your circumstances are. Life can be hard, and instead of just enduring it, embrace it, for it is a gift. Your life has a purpose. Each day is a new day, not just a continuation of yesterday. You must look at life in this way. Be encouraged that it is never to late to begin something you have always wanted to do.

"Efforts and courage are not enough without purpose and direction."
- *John F. Kennedy*

Perseverance

Perseverance and patience, these are magic words. They are the "Open Sesame" of our modern life. They open the door to opportunity and will bring you prosperity, peace, and plenty.

Therefore, courage, patience, and perseverance are to be your chief asset.

In 1492, Christopher Columbus landed on an island, which he thought was India.

Chris was mighty happy as he put his foot on good old mother earth, not so much because he had discovered a new way to India, as he thought, but because his foot touched land.

Two days before he landed on San Salvador, his crew grew angry with him and threatened to throw him into the sea and turn back with the ship to Spain. If Christopher had shown fear to those men, 1492 would not be the date of the very first line in geography books, announcing the "Discovery of America." He had real perseverance, the stuff that makes men successful. He started to find India by sailing westward. He didn't succeed in his purpose, but his determination was rewarded just the same, for he found a new country, and that was worthwhile.

Before he started, he was promised ten percent of the revenue from any lands he might discover. Just imagine what that would mean today.

The world has improved since 1492, but the percentage of men who would keep everlastingly at it like Columbus did, increases as the years pass.

Columbus sailed with three ships, the largest sixty-six feet long. He steered in the direction of the setting sun.

His crew was of one hundred and twenty men. None of them were very enthusiastic at the start; all of them were quite disgusted, discouraged and ready to mutiny. But Christopher kept the ships pointed westward, through rain and shine, through drifting, breezeless days and through wild stormy nights.

He kept on and on and on, and he brought home the bacon, success crowned his efforts. It was the mileage made on October 12th, 1492, that counted. It is the last step in a race that counts.

The moral is that many a prize has been lost just when it was ready to be plucked. Innovation distinguishes between a leader and a follower.

I had the pleasure of meeting Steve Jobs with his son, face to face as he waited for a pizza at my favorite Italian restaurant "Il Fornaio" in Palo Alto, CA. Steve Jobs and his dream is responsible for countless peoples careers in our generation. I find his quote caring and inspirational:

Being the richest man in the cemetery doesn't matter to me. Going to bed at night saying we've done something wonderful, that's what matters to me.
- Steve Jobs (1991–2011)

Many success stories like Apple, Facebook and other social networking sites on the web all started with an idea.

Each of us has a share in this world's work. It matters little whether our actual share is what we had guessed or wished it to be. Once one of your ideas is shared with others in a meeting or a team, the idea becomes all of yours.

So make sure to keep it secret or have them sign an NDA if you want all the credit.

The failure of past dreams should not grieve you. We cannot reach up and grasp the stars, but like a Captain at the helm on the open sea, we can navigate by those stars to help us on our way.

Our ideal may not be realized, but the journey to it may still be a pleasant one. If our ideas, plans, and hopes have a good purpose and offer a service, they will give us courage and will be worthwhile.

The brain cells grow in response to desire. Where there is no desire there is no growth. The brain develops most in the direction of the leading ambition, where the mental activities are the most pronounced.

The desire for a musical career, for instance, develops the musical brain cells.

Business ambition develops that part of the brain, which has to do with business, the cells which are brought into action in executive management and administering affairs in money making. Wherever we make our demand upon the brain by desire, that part will respond in growth.

We are beginning to realize that all of our experiences during the day, all of our thoughts, emotions and mental attitudes, which seem to make but a fleeting impression are not in reality lost but retained.

Now, it's worth repeating, if you are trying to be successful you must act like a successful person, carry yourself like one, talk, act and think like a winner. You must radiate victory wherever you go. You must maintain your attitude by believing in the thing you are trying to do.

By a psychological law, we attract that which corresponds with our mental attitude and with our faith with our hopes, expectations, doubts, and fears.
We attract what we love and also what we fear. If this were fully understood, and used as a working principle in life, we would have no poverty, no failures and perhaps no criminals. We would not see people everywhere with expressions indicating that there is very little enjoyment in living.

Every day leaves its phonographic recordings on the brain like the grooves in a record, and these records are never erased or destroyed. They simply drop into the subconscious mind and are ever on call. They may not come at once in response to our summons, but they are still there and are often, many years after they have dropped into the subconscious mind, reproduced with all their original vividness.

In our active days, we should realize that we are putting memories away in our mind and heart that will come back to us in old age.

Only that which we put in our mind and heart can we take out. So, build up loving ties, gratefulness, worthwhile riches of good deeds, and in the evening of your life, you will always be welcome wherever you go. To prepare for that happy period of your life, the foundation must be built in the active hours of today.

Think vital thoughts of courage, faith, and hope. Then your days will pass joyfully, and your path will be one of peace, happiness, and contentment. Think of wonderful memories and smile.

If you fill your mind with gloom and sorrowful thoughts, your surroundings will reflect your mental attitude and will accentuate your misery. Do not give in to a weak and depressed way of thinking. Always remind yourself to take your thoughts captive and throw out the bad ones.

You can be strong if you learn to control your thought habits. Take those thoughts captive. Many famous individuals have been credited with versions of the following quote:

> *"Watch your thoughts,*
> *They become words;*
> *Watch your words,*
> *They become actions;*
> *Watch your actions,*

They become habits;
Watch your habits,
They become character;
Watch your character,
For it becomes your destiny. "

Remember that destiny is by choice not by chance.

Do not think that you can go through life without your share of pain, disillusion, and disappointment. No man or woman has ever done it. Clouds will come, but they can be dispelled. Troubles will come but meet them boldly and courageously and do not show fear. Our unfulfilled expectations can only bring even more disappointment, learn to live with hope and faith, try to have less expectations of others and you will then find yourself more free of disappointment and anger. Life is a great arena where good and bad, joy and sorrow, faith and fear, happiness and unhappiness, success and failure are inescapable.

The joy and happiness, accept graciously, bear your sorrow with patience, keep faith in your heart and mind always.

Turn your fears into faith and grateful thoughts; remember fear and gratefulness cannot co-exist. Although it is not possible to enjoy an absolute and continued state of happiness, it always lies within your power to have serenity, poise, peace, and contentment.

We are just beginning to see that faith is as much a real force as electricity. It is faith that removes mountains of difficulty, opposition, and distrust. It clears the track of all obstructions. Faith is the most powerful, the most sublime of human attributes. Without it, the bottom would drop out of civilization. It is the divine fundamental principle of life. Having faith is the basis of health, success, happiness, and love itself. It believes, hopes, trusts and clings to the loved one in spite of all faults and sins. It is faith that heals, achieves and hopes.

The very feeling of unquestionable harmony between God and us is one that gives a sense of protection, which nothing else can give. You can pray for more faith and you will receive it.

Faith opens the doors to all things we desire in life and doubt closes them. No one can rise higher than his faith. No one can do a greater thing than he believes he can. The fact that a person believes that he can do what may seem impossible to others, shows there is something within him that has gotten a glimpse of power sufficient to accomplish his purpose. There is no doubt that every human being comes to this earth with a mission. We are not accidental puppets thrown to the earth by chance. We are all a part of the great universal plan. I believe we were made to play a definite part in it.

Life is short, and we have all come here with a message for humanity which no one else but ourselves can deliver. With faith in our mission and the belief that we are important factors in the great creative plan, that we are in fact, co-creators with God, will add wonderfully to the dignity and effectiveness of our lives, enabling us to perform the "impossible."

That is a lot to think about but it is so important to believe in the infinite possibilities and stay positive. We can choose to stop being negative or feeling sorry for ourselves. Think mostly cheerful thoughts and think of the good things that life has given you, not the least of them being life itself. Thinking of yourself as habitually lucky will tend to make you so, just as thinking of yourself as habitually unlucky and always talking about your failures and your cruel fate will tend to make you unlucky.

The attitude of your mind, which your thoughts and convictions produce, is a powerful force, which builds or tears down. The habit of always seeing yourself as a fortunate individual, the feeling grateful just for being alive, for being allowed to live on this beautiful earth and to have a chance to make good, will put your mind in a creative, producing attitude.

We should all go through life as though we were sent here with a sublime mission to lift, to help, to boost, and not to depress and discourage, and so discredit the plan of the Creator. Our conduct should show that we are on this earth to play a magnificent part in life's drama, to make a wonderful contribution to humanity. "As above, so below..." but is that what we truly see, heavenly perfection unfolding and playing out upon this earthly plane?

The fact that the answer to this generation is so different for each person makes the best case for "why" this book had to be written.

Only to the Beautiful Thinking person is the advantage given to see life and see it whole, keeping an eye on the main objective, secure in the realization that we are master of ourselves and the captain of our own soul. The "mind's eye" is responsible for all that we see, internally and externally. Care should be taken as to what we feed it.

The practice of "Beautiful Thinking" is a tower of strength. If you are a thinker, life's little troubles serve but to reinforce your spirit of resistance and make you stronger.

So then, by all means, think, for it is by Beautiful Thinking that the future joy and happiness and peace of the world must be increased. Only we can change our world. It all starts in our mind and heart.

Some *quotes* to think about and live by...

"Imagine yourself as a living house. God comes in to rebuild that house. At first, perhaps, you can understand what He is doing. He is getting the drains right and stopping the leaks in the roof and so on; you knew that those jobs needed doing

and so you are not surprised. But presently He starts knocking the house about in a way that hurts abominably and does not seem to make any sense. What on earth is He up to? The explanation is that He is building quite a different house from the one you thought of - throwing out a new wing here, putting on an extra floor there, running up towers, making courtyards. You thought you were being made into a decent little cottage: but He is building a palace. He intends to come and live in it Himself."
- *C.S. Lewis*

If you tell the truth you don't have to remember anything.
- *Mark Twain*

Keep true, never be ashamed of doing right, decide on what you think is right and stick to it.
- *George Eliot*

Character is what you are in the dark.
- *Dwight L. Moody*

Nearly all men can stand adversity, but if you want to test a man's character, give him power.
- *Abraham Lincoln*

It takes less time to do a thing right than to explain why you did it wrong.
- *Henry Wadsworth Longfellow*

The true perfection of man lies not in what man has, but in what man is.
- *Oscar Wilde*

Whoever is careless with the truth in small matters cannot be trusted with important matters.
- *Albert Einstein*

Anger is one letter short of danger.
- *Eleanor Roosevelt*

Anger is an acid that can do more harm to the vessel in which it is stored than to anything on which it is poured.
- *Mark Twain*

It is wise to direct your anger towards problems -- not people; to focus your energies on answers -- not excuses.
- *William Arthur Ward*

We're born alone, we live alone, we die alone. Only through our love and friendship can we create the illusion for the moment that we're not alone.
- *Orson Welles*

Without great solitude no serious work is possible.
- *Pablo Picasso*

I used to think that the worst thing in life was to end up all alone. It's not. The worst thing in life is ending up with people who make you feel all-alone.
- *Robin Williams*

The talent for being happy is appreciating and liking what you have, instead of what you don't have.
- *Woody Allen*

Doing what you like is freedom. Liking what you do is happiness.
- *Frank Tyger*

Happiness cannot be traveled to, owned, earned, worn or consumed. Happiness is the spiritual experience of living every minute with love, grace, and gratitude.
- *Denis Waitley*

If you want to be happy, be.
- *Leo Tolstoy*

Happiness is the meaning and the purpose of life, the whole aim and end of human existence.
- *Aristotle*

The best way to cheer yourself up is to try to cheer somebody else up.
- *Mark Twain*

Dream as if you'll live forever, live as if you'll die today.
- *James Dean*
Each morning when I open my eyes I say

to myself: I, not events, have the power to make me happy or unhappy today. I can choose how I feel and act towards others. Yesterday is dead and tomorrow hasn't arrived yet. I have just one day, today, and I'm going to be happy in it.
- *Groucho Marx*

I have learned now that while those who speak about one's miseries usually hurt, those who keep silence hurt more.
- *C.S. Lewis*

Just because somebody is strong enough to handle pain doesn't mean they deserve it.
- *unknown*

Happiness is like a butterfly which, when pursued, is always beyond our grasp, but, if you will sit down quietly, it may alight upon you.
- *Nathaniel Hawthorne*

Everyone thinks of changing the world, but no one thinks of changing himself.

- Leo Tolstoy

Knowing others is intelligence; knowing yourself is true wisdom. Mastering others is strength; mastering yourself is true power.
- Lao-Tzu

We must accept finite disappointment, but never lose infinite hope.
- Martin Luther King, Jr.

Hope is being able to see that there is light despite all of the darkness.
- Desmond Tutu

Start by doing what's necessary; then do what's possible, and suddenly you are doing the impossible.
- Francis of Assisi

"One can have no smaller or greater mastery than mastery of oneself."
- Leonardo da Vinci

Remember happiness doesn't depend upon who you are or what you have; it depends solely on what you think.
- *Dale Carnegie*

Change your thoughts and you change your world.
- *Norman Vincent Peale*

Beauty is a radiance that originates from within and comes from inner security and strong character.
- *Jane Seymour*

Love is patient, love is kind. It does not envy, it does not boast, it is not proud. It does not dishonor others, it is not self-seeking, it is not easily angered, it keeps no record of wrongs. Love does not delight in evil but rejoices with the truth. It always protects, always trusts, always hopes, always perseveres.
- *1 Corinthians 13:4-7*

"When the heart is beautiful, its light shines through the eyes, vocal tones and

actions of its master. True beauty is not in the body, but in the heart of the beholder."
- *Suzy Kassem*

"Beauty is not in the face; beauty is a light in the heart."
- *Kahlil Gibran*

It is during our darkest moments that we must focus to see the light.
- *Aristotle*

"Inner Beauty in itself is a life manual of sorts which every age group can find applicable, as loving yourself never has an expiration date. As an eighteen-year old college student, this chapter speaks to me in volumes as the issues of hope, faith, judgement and self-love are addressed so personally and realistically. I am so thankful for Tricia's spoken and written wisdom, as she truly is a mentor to me and always manages to spread joy."
- *Adriana Ferrari*

My Thoughts

I wanted to add that the reason I studied these inspirational books from the late 1800's and early 1900's is because I lost my parents as a teen and needed much guidance. I found it in books. Some of us have parents that gave or give us guidance and direction, and some still living have not and still do not. Those of you that had guidance, you are blessed indeed.

Our children and teens are witnessing adults behaving badly in the world today and it's not helping to mentor them

In the past as in the present, I feel the world has been breaking apart and all of our hearts are breaking right along with it. We all are affected by the manmade and natural disasters globally.

We are all witnessing the actions of our Politicians who are responsible for creating division, along with their followers who write outrageous comments on social media for all to see and comment on. These diverse groups are filled with hate, and have caused more chaos than any of us had ever imagined.

All I can do is share the words, thoughts and experiences in this book so that you might understand how many of life's obstacles are not brought on by our own doing, but things sometimes just happen to us. It is up to us on how we react or respond to circumstances.

Let us act with compassion and teach each other how to have Beautiful Thinking by our actions and our words.

Life is short and what we do here on this earth can make a difference, even if it's only in our own home. After all, love is all we need and what really matters most in the world. We all want true love and to be loved.

Acknowledgements

Thank you to my family and my wonderful friends and clients for all your advice and your encouragement.

Thank you to my favorite editor, Hamilton Wordsworth you are a real peach.

Thank you to Joan Falkenstein for taking the time to perfect my punctuation in this book.

Thank you to Mel Lindstrom for the photos on the cover of the book at melphoto.com. After knowing you almost forty years, you still rock... my friend.

Thank you to Matthew Dovel, Author of, "My Last Breath" for your words of instruction and wisdom for the chapter, "The Storm of Depression"

Thank you to Heather Haven for your thoughts and review on the back of my book.

BIBLIOGRAPHY

James Allen (1864 - 1912)
A British philosophical writer known for his inspirational books, poetry and was a pioneer of the self-help movement.

Dr. Orison Swett Marden (1848–1924)
An American inspirational author, who wrote about achieving success in life and founded *Success* magazine in 1897

Col. WM. C. Hunter (1866 -?)
A successful businessman, and self-help writer, who was popular in the early 20th century. His books set forth his personal philosophy on health, happiness, human relations, and success in the business world.

Alexander, James W. (1804-1859)
Was an American Presbyterian minister and a theologian.

www.ingramcontent.com/pod-product-compliance
Lightning Source LLC
Chambersburg PA
CBHW041819090426

42811CB00009B/1038